ALWAYS AT ODDS?

ALWAYS AT ODDS?

Creating Alignment between Faculty and Administrative Values

MARY C. WRIGHT

STATE UNIVERSITY OF NEW YORK PRESS

MT

Cover: *Alternative View*, sculpture by Mark Chatterley,
ceramic and steel, 60 x 72 x 12 inches, n.d.
Photograph by Sculpturesite Gallery, San Francisco, CA. Used by permission.

Frank and Ernest cartoon © 2004 Thaves. Reprinted with permission.

Published by
STATE UNIVERSITY OF NEW YORK PRESS, ALBANY

© 2008 State University of New York

Printed in the United States of America

For information, contact State University of New York Press, Albany, NY
www.sunypress.edu

Production, Laurie Searl
Marketing, Anne M. Valentine

Library of Congress Cataloging-in-Publication Data

Wright, Mary, 1971–
    Always at odds : creating alignment between faculty and administration values / Mary
Wright.
        p. cm.
    Includes bibliographical references and index.
    ISBN 978-0-7914-7367-2 (hardcover : alk. paper)
    ISBN 978-0-7914-7368-9 (pbk. : alk. paper)
    1. Universities and colleges—United States—Faculty—Attitudes. 2. Teacher-
administrator relationships—United States. 3. Universities and colleges—United States—
Administration. 4. Communication in education—United States. I. Title.

LB2331.72.W75 2008
378.1'2—dc22   2007024501

10 9 8 7 6 5 4 3 2 1

11/05/08

to Russ and Laurea

CONTENTS

TABLES

ACKNOWLEDGMENTS

I would like to thank the social networks who helped support me in the completion of this book: my family, Russ, Laurea, Theresa, and Ken; my dissertation committee, Jan Lawrence, Al Young, and Pat Shure, and a special thanks to my chair, Mark Chesler; my colleagues at the Center for Research on Learning and Teaching, especially its director, Connie Cook; the supportive mentors I met through the July 2000 American Sociological Association Workshop on the Scholarship of Teaching and Learning; and friends who commented on early drafts, such as Joel Purkiss, Julica Hermann, and Susannah Dolance. I also thank the fantastic and encouraging sociology professors I had as an undergraduate, especially Gene Burns and Kristen Luker. Many thanks to Mark Chatterley and Sculpturesite Gallery for the image of the provocative sculpture, "Alternative View," which appears on the cover. Finally, my utmost gratitude is extended to the faculty and chairs who took the time to speak to me about their work for this project.

CHAPTER ONE

INTRODUCTION

In *The courage to teach*, sociologist and educational lecturer Parker Palmer (1998, pp. 173–174) describes a typical incident on his lecture tour:

> When my opening talk is over, someone will come up to me and confide, "I agree with everything you say about teaching—but I am the only person on campus who feels this way." At the end of the second session, three or four more people will approach me, one by one to share the same secret. By the time I leave, I have met ten or fifteen people who share a common vision for education—each of whom is certain that he or she is alone on this campus.

Paralleling Palmer's observations, survey data of research university faculty indicate that there are curious discrepancies in the value that faculty assign to teaching and the worth they believe their colleagues and organizations attribute to instructional activities. A study of faculty in eleven research and doctoral institutions in 1991 and 1996 found that faculty felt they attributed more importance to teaching than did their departmental colleagues, chairs, deans and central administrators (Diamond & Adam, 1997). A 1980 study of faculty at a large public university reported that 98 percent of faculty attach considerable or great importance to teaching, and 83 percent would rate their own teaching above average or superior. However, when it came to assessment of colleagues, 73 percent thought their colleagues gave much weight to teaching, and only 52 percent rated their colleagues' teaching highly (Blackburn et al., 1980). Recent qualitative research points to similar incongruities (Lindholm, 2003; Wood & Des Jarlais, 2006).

Why is the presence of the fit between an individual's own values and perceptions of organizational priorities important? Research indicates that compared to other professionals, faculty are more likely to experience fulfillment when there is an alignment between their own and organizational

1

values—and strain when there is a mismatch (Schuster & Finkelstein, 2006). As a result, congruence is associated with outcomes that every faculty member and academic administrator wishes upon his or her organization: increased job satisfaction, lower attrition, better job performance, and a strengthened commitment to the organization (Chatman, 1991; Chatman & Barsade, 1995; Kristof-Brown, Zimmerman, & Johnson, 2005; O'Reilly, Chatman, & Caldwell, 1991; Verquer, Beeher, & Wagner, 2002). In the university context, faculty who perceive themselves to be at odds with their department or institution's organizational climate indicate higher levels of job-related stress, report less overall satisfaction with their positions, and spend less time on teaching (Blackburn & Lawrence, 1995; Fairweather & Rhoads, 1995; Olsen, Maple, & Stage, 1995; Peters & Mayfield, 1982).

However, person-organization misfit in regard to instructional beliefs, or the pattern of rating one's own value of teaching above peers', is not found among faculty in other institutional types, such as in two-year colleges or master's institutions (Blackburn & Lawrence, 1995). Uniquely, faculty in research universities tend to hold views about teaching that they feel are incongruent with those of their peers, supervisors, and institution.

What is it about a research university that would produce lack of agreement between the individual's values and perceptions of organizational leaders' views? Within one research university, why might some departments' responses run counter to this trend, indicating a consensus about the value of teaching? In this book, I explore research university departments in which there is *instructional congruence*, or a culture in which individuals perceive that their beliefs about teaching align with their institution. These department members have constructed shared understandings of effective teaching and the value they place on instruction.[1] I also examine academic units that have a culture of incongruence, in which members feel that they disagree with the organization's and their colleagues' stance(s) on teaching.

In this book, I address the following questions: What is it about a research university that would produce lack of agreement between the individual's and the institution's values? Within one research university, why might some departments' responses run counter to this trend, indicating a consensus about the value of teaching? Finally, what can chairs, faculty, and faculty developers who wish to create a congruent teaching culture do?

In the chapters that follow, I offer four general prerequisites for a culture of congruence: (1) the presence of interpretive structures, or shared instantiation of teaching guidelines, which arise because of (2) clear and transparent formal instructional policies that promote interaction around teaching, (3) practices that facilitate widespread faculty instructional networks, and (4) communication between faculty and chairs. Each of these dynamics forms the basis of a chapter.

This approach is based on both an interactionist and an interactive view of organizations, generally, and of academic departments, specifically

(Moran & Volkwein, 1992).[2] It sees congruence as arising from a relationship between "objective" structures, such as policies that govern teaching, and "subjective" interpretations of those policies, which develop from social interaction, or opportunities to talk about teaching.

Congruence entails a shared value of the worth of teaching in faculty work, but it is important to state that congruence does not imply uniformity. Congruent departments need not be comprised of instructional clones, who all teach alike. However, for congruence, or alignment about the value of teaching, to exist in a department, faculty will have a *repertoire* of shared understandings about what constitutes effective teaching and how to assess it.

Although the book focuses on instructional congruence, readers also may find applications to other institutional settings, such as liberal arts college departments where there are discussions about the value of research (Krebs, 2005), parts of a campus that would like others to value public scholarship (Cantor & Lavine, 2006), or departments that are divided by disagreements about other values. Across institutions, faculty's sense of community and satisfaction with administration is on the decline, and this book focuses on possible influences on these trends (Schuster & Finkelstein, 2006). Additionally, this work also will hold implications for those seeking to enhance *research* productivity in their departments, as many of the organizational structures and informal practices that I highlight are shared by scholarship that examines building blocks of effective research cultures (Bilmoria & Jordan, 2005; Bland, Weber-Main, Lund, & Finstad, 2005).

RESEARCH UNIVERSITIES

In 1970, the Carnegie Foundation for the Advancement of Teaching Commission on Higher Education first constructed its classification of postsecondary institutions. As commission chair Clark Kerr explained: "We sought to identify categories of colleges and universities that would be relatively homogenous with respect to the functions of the institutions as well as with respect to characteristics of students and faculty members" (Carnegie Commission on Higher Education, 1973). Five institutional categories emerged from subsequent Carnegie classifications—doctoral/research universities, master's colleges and universities, baccalaureate colleges, associate's colleges, and specialized institutions—based on degrees offered, federal support dollars, and the specialized mission of the institution. (More recently, the classification has been modified to add additional dimensions—such as community engagement and an enrollment profile—but the "basic classification" remains similar: doctorate-granting universities, master's institutions, baccalaureate colleges, associate's colleges, and special focus institutions.) Over the years it has been in existence, the Carnegie classification has come to signal selectivity, stringency of tenure requirements, research focus, and prestige, with doctoral/research universities at the pinnacle of this system. ("Doctoral/

research universities" and "doctorate-granting universities" are henceforth called "research universities.")

However, when it comes to teaching—a factor not yet measured by the Carnegie classification—research universities popularly are placed near the bottom of the scale. The widely read *U.S. News and World Report* rankings issue headlined, "Research Universities *Are Working* to Put Undergraduates First" (italics added), indicating that they are not yet quite there (Marcus, 1999). A recent college guidebook steers prospective applicants to small, lesser known liberal arts colleges, advising, "Since research and publishing are where all the rewards are, the top faculty at leading universities do little, if any, teaching, leaving that chore to graduate assistants and part-time faculty. In short, the university cheats the undergraduate" (Pope, 1996, p. 3).

Despite these indicators that research institutions may not prioritize student learning, in surveys that ask research university professors if they value teaching, most say that they do (Blackburn et al., 1980; Diamond & Adam, 1997). Additionally, in recent decades, many research universities have moved to enhance the value placed on teaching, even if they do not concurrently decrease the emphasis allocated to research and service (Wright, Howery, Assar, McKinney, Kain, Glass, Kramer, & Atkinson, 2004). Finally, most surveys of research faculty's use of their time still find a greater proportion is spent on teaching than on research activities (Schuster & Finkelstein, 2006). Therefore, what may be most unique about a research university is not the value it or its faculty place on teaching, but the incongruent views held about instruction, a misalignment that hinders faculty professional development and departmental growth.

However, research on individual disciplines hints that these institutional-level patterns may conceal important exceptions within a university, with some fields tending to agree more about teaching matters than others. There is more disciplinary variation on the value of teaching as a promotion criterion within a research university than in any other institutional type (Leslie, 2002). As a result, studies that focus only on the institutional level may mask important variations in faculty beliefs. For example, disciplines in which faculty tend to agree on research-oriented questions—e.g., appropriate research methods, research questions, and theoretical scaffoldings—also tend to show higher levels of agreement about instructional matters, such as appropriate course content and teaching expectations (Braxton & Berger, 1999; Braxton & Hargens, 1996; Lattuca & Stark, 1995).

However, what these studies do not indicate is why these variations arise. Are they are attributable to unique aspects of disciplinary cultures? Common organizational structures that facilitate attitudinal agreement? Socialization patterns? For example, agreement may result from a discipline's tendency simply to see eye to eye about research and instructional techniques, due to common socialization, or it may stem from a pattern of instructional arrangements that overlaps significantly with faculty's research responsibilities, or from other influences. This book examines the particular nature of the factors that produce agreement about teaching matters in some departments and disagreement in others. It puts particular emphasis on the important role the academic department plays, an important space where faculty work gets done, but one that is often overlooked in university reform efforts (Edwards, 1999).

AMBIGUITY

In their classic 1958 study, Caplow and McGee (pp. 135–136) documented that the absence of requirements for instructional effectiveness creates a climate in which the only standard for teaching is attainment of the doctorate:

> Where men [and women] are hired to teach only on the basis of their research productivity, what happens to teaching? With the exception of some humanities departments and a few atypical natural science and social science departments, the answer to this query takes two general forms: (1) Teaching doesn't matter—it isn't important; and (2) There's nothing to worry about—any Ph.D. can teach.

Unlike research activities, with their well-structured public forums of peer review, conference presentations, funding decisions, and yearly reports, there are few common references for research faculty to evaluate pedagogy.

Today, teaching still largely remains a "private affair" (Seldin, 1990, p.5). Because of this lack of collective engagement around teaching, ideas about what constitutes "adequate" teaching—and even definitions of the activity (e.g., Is teaching: work in classrooms? one-on-one work with students on a research project? advising?)—contribute to an environment where instructional standards are opaque and often contradictory. Although increasingly more attention is being given to teaching in research universities, they continue to present more ambiguity over institutional messages about teaching expectations and norms than other types of institutions (Braxton, Bayer, & Finkelstein, 1992; Braxton & Berger, 1999; Quinn, 1994; Woods, 1999). Studies of how research university professors define "effective teaching" indicate that there is a wide variety of meanings attributed to the work, including lecturing, keeping abreast of disciplinary content, being enthusiastic, improving students' higher-order thinking, facilitating student learning, and conveying facts (Blackburn, Boberg, O'Connell, & Pellino, 1980; Boice, 1991, 1992; Fink, 1984; Goodwin & Stevens, 1993; Mann, 1970). Methods for evaluating teaching have been called idiosyncratic and unsystematic (Tierney & Bensimon, 1996).

There are many reasons why the research university creates such an ambiguous institutional context around the issue of teaching. Researchers name several characteristics of ambiguous and changing situations, all of which are represented in the research university context (March & Olsen, 1976; McCaskey, 1982).

First, there exist inconsistent and ill-defined objectives about teaching. Most research universities establish and maintain few clear, shared criteria for good teaching (Tierney & Bensimon, 1996). When asked, "How important are observations of your teaching by colleagues and/or administrators for granting tenure in your department?," compared to faculty in all institutional types, those in research universities were least likely to find it important (Boyer, 1990). In their sample of tenure and promotion policies at representative colleges and universities nationwide, the Harvard Project on Faculty Appointments found no Research I institutions that required a classroom observation (O'Meara, 2000).[3] These findings indicate that faculty and administrators in research universities lack or reject opportunities to gather direct evidence on teaching standards and approaches. This information would assist faculty in establishing shared understandings of the constituents of effective teaching.

Second, goals and responsibilities in ambiguous scenarios are unclear or multiple and conflicting. New faculty frequently express frustration in the unstated expectations of the teaching role, often because research universities already assume that they know how to teach (Tierney & Rhoads, 1993; Whitt, 1991). What "causes" one to get tenure or why others in the department were denied is not easily understood. Faculty report that assessment of teaching for tenure is "based on individual and particularistic notions that reveal more about the idiosyncrasies of the evaluator than about a communal agreement as to what constitutes good teaching" (Tierney & Bensimon, 1996, p. 65).

Social psychologists have long understood that ambiguous criteria for judgment and limited communication lead individuals to misgauge their beliefs in relation to others', whether through self-serving appraisals (Alicke et al., 1985; Dunning et al., 1989; Van Lange, 1991), uniqueness effects (Campbell, 1986; Goethals, 1986; Marks & Miller, 1987), or pluralistic ignorance (Hofer & Brown, 1992; Miller & McFarland, 1987; Miller & Prentice, 1996). Each of these concepts indicates that if faculty are not exposed to clear standards for teaching and do not engage in further discussion about what those standards would mean for the particular department, faculty can be expected to believe that their values differ from peers and supervisors.

Imagine a busy pedestrian walkway: some people are moving along on bicycles, others with skates, still others on foot. Everyone is going someplace; this much is evident. However, who is going where? Who is using the most effective mode of transportation? Who spends most time and effort getting to his or her destination? What is the *best* way to get from point A to B? Each traveler's answer to this question is different. However, at selected times, driven by traffic patterns or clear directions from strategically placed signposts, even busy pedestrians may be directed to come together and proceed along effective pathways.

In a manner similar to this hectic avenue, each faculty member in a research university travels on a particular instructional pathway, some with "vehicles" (e.g., techniques, expertise, commitments) that are more efficient than others. In most cases, each professor travels in isolation, relying upon his/her own ideas and guesses about what works in the classroom and how much priority should be allocated to teaching. However, in selected contexts, shaped by opportunities for social interaction and understandings about instructional policies, faculty can develop a sense that the value they accord to teaching and the ways "good teaching" is defined are congruent with their postsecondary institution.

THIS STUDY

The study takes place at a large research university, classified as a "Research University—Extensive" in the Carnegie typology. Indeed, the institution could be termed the archetypical research university, as at the time of the study it was among the top postsecondary institutions in the United States in terms of money spent on research and scholarly work. To select departments within the university, I utilized results from a 1996 survey of faculty on work-life issues that was conducted by an on-campus administrative unit. The survey was sent to 2,624 individuals in January 1996; its population consisted of all faculty who held at least half-time instructional appointments, who had been at the university for at least a year, and who were in tenured, tenure-track, advanced clinical, or lecturer positions. There was a response rate of 44 percent, with a fairly even representation of academic divisions.

Twelve of the university's academic units were selected through a "congruence index," which measured alignment about teaching-related issues among faculty in a given unit. This index was comprised of two components: the first focused on preferences for work allocation and the second on standards for effective teaching. As a measure of agreement about the value placed on teaching by faculty and their perceptions of administrative policies, the percentage of time respondents preferred to spend with students (on teaching and advising) was compared with the percentage of time they thought their units wanted them to allocate. Second, to measure the alignment between individual and group definitions of teaching effectiveness, for each department the percentage of faculty that said effective teaching was somewhat or highly characteristic of valued colleagues was subtracted from the percentage of faculty that indicated that effective teaching was somewhat or highly characteristic of them personally.[4] To create the congruence index, the absolute value of both of these percentages (time and effective teaching) was taken, and they were summed. A value of zero indicated that survey respondents perceived an alignment between their own and departmental decision makers' desired emphasis on instruction, while a large positive percentage signaled that individuals perceive different priorities.

Six departments with the lowest sums (ranging from 1.7 percent to 4.7 percent) were selected as possible congruent cases, and six departments with the highest sums (from 54.1 percent to 80.0 percent) were chosen as possible incongruent cases; all of the resulting units were in the sciences or health sciences.[5] This quantitative approach to case selection was supplemented with a qualitative screening, to focus on four departments that were roughly matched by size and emphasis on undergraduate or graduate/professional instruction.

While the cases for this project were selected quantitatively, the main research data for this study were qualitative. This study was organized in two waves: in the first section, junior faculty were interviewed. The purpose of these interviews was to map whom respondents talked to about teaching, recheck departments' levels of congruence/incongruence, and understand what structures, policies, and/or practices might be influencing the presence of congruence/incongruence. (See Appendix A for the interview instrument.) Junior faculty were the primary focus because they are the rank most likely to be new to the organization, and therefore would have a fresh perspective on its environment. Through the process of entry into the position, new faculty's socialization experiences can highlight the values, beliefs, norms for practice, and expectations of the department, or, as one scholar of organizational culture succinctly puts it, "How we do things and what matters around here" (Louis, 1980, p. 232). Because assistant professors have not yet been through the tenure decision, they face the most ambiguity over that process. This ambiguity is useful for uncovering respondents' tacit understandings of culture, because when faced with ambiguity, processes of sense making, interpretation, and reliance on preexisting cognitive frameworks are maximized (Sackmann, 1991).

In the first wave of the study, all junior faculty in the four departments were contacted, and more than 80 percent (N=17) took part in a forty-minute semi-structured interview. Based on these respondents' recommendations about whom they talk to about teaching, I gathered sixty-one other faculty names of faculty (including eleven assistant professor peers) and faculty-administrators.

In the second wave, I contacted at least one person from every assistant professor's list (if there was one) and every person who was named at least two times. Because I intended to analyze the data using a grounded theory approach, a tenet of which is to select interview subjects based on how they will contribute to conceptual frameworks, I also looked to fill in gaps, such as by rank, gender, race/ethnicity, or instructional emphasis. From these contacts, I interviewed twenty-nine associate, full, and emeritus professors. Many of them had been at the university for a longer time and had held important administrative positions, and therefore, they were important sources of information about departmental histories and policies. Additionally, as more senior department members who had been referenced as important members of the assistant professors' instructional reference group, I looked to this second wave of interviews for an understanding of how they might influence the junior faculty's views on teaching.

These interviews, and all other data from assistant professors' interviews, were analyzed using grounded theory. Because of the paucity of empirically based theoretical frameworks regarding beliefs about teaching, an inductive methodology promised to elicit the most valuable insights (Clark & Peterson, 1986; Sackmann, 1991). Grounded theory was selected because it is one of the better established inductive methodological frameworks, useful for its established procedures for generating theory, hypotheses, and concepts from data (Charmaz, 1983; Glaser, 1987; Glaser & Strauss, 1967). Interviews were transcribed and coded with NVivo, a qualitative analysis program, using an approach that falls somewhere between a line-by-line *in vivo* method (Chesler, 1987) and a very broad, conceptual lens (Corbin & Strauss, 1990; Glaser, 1987).

Finally, in the last wave of interviews, conducted near the end of the project, I spoke with lead administrators in all of the four departments. (See Appendix B for the interview instrument.) These interviews served as "member checks," soliciting feedback on major themes and findings developed in each of the case studies (Lincoln & Guba, 1985). (Findings were presented in the aggregate with deliberate care not to reveal identities of faculty respondents who participated in earlier phases of the study.) Additionally, because the role of the chair and other key administrators emerged as a theme in earlier interviews, I also solicited their perspective on how they understood and carried out their duties.

In total, I interviewed forty-six faculty and four lead administrators.[6] In Table 1, the aggregate and departmentally specific numbers of *faculty* respondents is presented. I interviewed about a quarter of faculty in three departments; in the graduate congruent department, because of its small size, I was

Table 1. Faculty Respondents by Department (% of Department's Faculty)

		Number of Faculty Respondents (Percent of Department's Full-Time Instructional Staff and Emeriti)
Graduate	Incongruent	8 (28%)
	Congruent	9 (64%)
Undergraduate	Incongruent	11 (22%)
	Congruent	18 (24%)

able to interview more than half. For each department, I made sure I achieved saturation before ending the interview process.

Table Two illustrates the breakdown by rank, indicating the number of faculty interviewed and the percentage of the department's faculty by each rank that this number comprises. Because this study focuses on the perspectives of junior faculty, more attention was devoted to recruitment of assistant and clinical assistant professors. Therefore, the proportion of junior faculty in each department ranges from 75 to 100 percent, while a lesser percentage of tenured professors was interviewed.

Overall, most of the respondents were white (80 percent) and male (83 percent). Although this was not a very diverse sample, it does resemble the populations of the departments in this study. At the time of this study, 82 pecent of tenured, tenure-track, and regular clinical instructional faculty at the university were identified as nonminorities, so the sample here mirrors the departments' demographics. Very few women (17 percent of all respondents) were interviewed, but the proportion in my study actually is an overrepresentation of the proportion of women in many of the departments, which ranges from 5 percent to 30 percent. (See table 8 in chapter 4 for more information on the gender composition of these departments.)

OTHER SOURCES OF DATA: DOCUMENTS, ARCHIVAL RECORDS, OBSERVATION, AND PHYSICAL ARTIFACTS

Because triangulation between multiple sources of data promises to verify findings, I utilized a number of other types of evidence for my study (Denzin, 1978). These included:

• *Documents*: I used a number of official documents in this research, including tenure and promotion policies, faculty directories, committee reports, course listings, and news articles from departments, division, or university sources. Many of these were accessible on the Web; some were fortuitously

Table 2. Number of Faculty Respondents by Rank (% of Department's Faculty in Rank)

		Rank				
		Asst.	*Assoc.*	*Full*	*Clinical*	*Emeritus*
Grad.	Incongruent	2 (75%)	0 (0%)	5 (28%)	N/A	1 (25%)
Departments	Congruent	3 (100%)	0 (100%)	3 (75%)	3 (100%)	0 (0%)
Undergrad.	Incongruent	6 (75%)	3 (38%)	2 (6%)	N/A	0 (0%)
Departments	Congruent	6 (100%)	2 (15%)	9 (21%)	N/A	1 (7%)
Total Respondents		17	5	19	3	2

gained because of the flurry of working committee reports released for the university's most recent accreditation.

• *Archival Records*: Many of the records that might have been useful for this study, such as recent personnel records, will be sealed for decades to come. However, the university archive did have some useful documents pertaining to the history of the four departments, such as records of external review reports. Additionally, in the case of the incongruent undergraduate department, I was able to use published histories of instructional decisions written by members of the unit and external researchers.

• *Observation*: I used this technique infrequently, but it did elicit interesting data. For example, I observed the activities and participants in some of the incongruent undergraduate department pedagogical seminars, and I gathered information during my "recruiting mission" at the congruent undergraduate unit's faculty meeting. Because I did not recognize many of the faculty at these gatherings, sometimes observations necessitated an "informant," who could identify participants for me.

• *Physical Artifacts*: Physical space played a more important role in this study than I originally had anticipated. The location of faculty's offices often played a key role in their opportunities to interact with peers on instructional matters. As a result, I made maps of hallways or took notes on office size or location so as to highlight the impact of physical structure on congruence and isolation.

A note about writing: As a condition of entry, departments were promised that I would not reveal details about their organizations that would directly identify them. As a result, many of the documents and archival records used cannot be specifically cited, as they are references that would identify the units. When this occurs, I try to give additional sources (e.g., quotes from respondents) to increase verification of the information.

DESCRIPTION OF DEPARTMENTS

To select the four cases, I sought to match a congruent unit with an incongruent unit. To ensure that these units could be appropriately compared, I paired departments by their undergraduate or postbaccalureate focus and their size.[7] The distinction between instructional emphases is important because of the qualitative differences between instruction at these two levels. While much of undergraduate teaching takes place in the classroom, graduate instruction often blurs research and teaching, in contexts such as a research laboratory or clinic setting. Size was also significant for this study on congruence, because an increased number of staff in a unit can lead to a less close-knit social structure (Friedkin, 1978).

In the case studies that follow in this book, the departments are labeled by meaningful identifiers, originating from respondents' descriptors of their departments (Table 3). One pair contains the incongruent "Star Department," named because there were star-shaped instructional networks, and the congruent "Universe Department," which offered more universal opportunities for interactions around instruction. Both were large (between fifty and seventy-five full-time instructional staff and emerti) science units that had significant undergraduate components. The other pair included the congruent unit, described by respondents as a well-functioning "Team Department," and the incongruent "Divided Department," which contained an interactional schism because of divisions in the type of teaching performed in the department. The Divided and Team Departments were two small health science departments (between fourteen and twenty-nine full-time instructional staff and emerti) that primarily offered postbaccalaureate education.

Departments' governance structures also were similar among the pairs. The larger science department chairs' decision-making capabilities often were delegated to assistant or associate chairs and were limited by executive committees with voting powers. These chairs conceptualized their role as democratic coordinators. In contrast, the heads of the much smaller health sciences units worked with advisory teams that had no voting powers. Although these units had section heads or directors, they did not have an assistant/associate chair structure to delegate responsibilities.

These four departments resided in three different meso-administrative units (analogous to a division, school, or college; henceforth, called colleges). Each department characterized their relationship with their respective college differently, and the units' policies (e.g., tenure and promotion) varied somewhat. However, the university is highly decentralized, and therefore each department shared a degree of autonomy from its college.

A traditional measure of good research is generalizability, but many qualitative research scholars find that more appropriate standards for case study research are applicability or transferability. This criterion asks the researcher to present rich detail about a case so that others can judge the fit of data/interpretations to their own contexts (Lincoln & Guba, 1985; Ragin, Nagel, & White, 2004). Therefore, in the remainder of this chapter, I offer an overview of each department's history, which serves as an important background for the chapters that follow. Chapter 3 goes into more detail about the official policies

Table 3. Code Names of Departments in the Study

	Congruent	Incongruent
Large, Undergraduate Focus	Universe Department	Star Department
Small, Postbaccalaureate Focus	Team Department	Divided Department

that are in place for evaluating teaching (and how faculty interpret them). Chapter 4 more extensively describes the teaching networks present in each unit, and it also depicts differing instructional arrangements.

Undergraduate Incongruent: Star Department

The Star Department scored as one of the more incongruent departments in the university. Founded in the mid-nineteenth century, it is one of the university's oldest and largest academic units on campus. This staffing level is matched by the number of students enrolled in the program, with the department awarding a large number of bachelor's degrees.

In recent years, the department faced a number of changes. First, the department has grown significantly, often through aggressive recruitment and retention of junior faculty. Second, beginning in the mid-1980s, the department was heavily involved in enhancing its undergraduate and graduate curriculum. According to one faculty-administrator, these reforms were prompted by enrollment concerns, or seeing "good talents going to other professions."

The process began in the mid-1980s with a four-year assessment and self-examination led by three faculty. After these first steps, the department held a retreat where faculty were asked to identify with one of the following positions:

- I believe that curricular change is necessary and I am willing to be involved in the process.

- I believe that curricular change is necessary, but I am unwilling to put any effort toward the process.

- I believe that curricular change is unnecessary.

Only about one-third chose active involvement, but administrators felt that there were sufficient numbers in the active reform camp to proceed with curricular change. Much of the actual work ended up being spearheaded by three faculty members: two have since retired while another continues to work for the university. The unit has been nationally recognized for this work.

In this book, this unit is titled the "Star Department," because work on these reforms and other teaching issues has been led by this remaining key unit member. I do not use the term *star* facetiously, but to reflect the "gravitational pull" that instructional activities have in reference to this key actor and the high visibility this person has both within and outside of the local university context. Additionally, the department's map of teaching interactions (chapter 4) approximates a star pattern, where there is centralization of information around one key actor (Moreno, 1934). It would be overstating the case to say that *all* activity around instructional issues is directed by "the star"; for example, one respondent was involved in an undergraduate course reform, and some others did significant work with graduate students. However, all of these people mentioned that they often consulted the "star" or worked under the auspices of the star's programs.

Overview of Teaching in the Star Department

In terms of the most traditional understanding of instructional work—classroom teaching—the standard full-time load for faculty with a research agenda was one course per term. In addition to this work in the classroom, the Star Department had a research requirement for undergraduates, in which they worked on a project under a faculty supervisor, often in a group with several graduate students and post-docs.

The largest enrollments took place in the introductory courses, and as one faculty member explained, "We see ourselves as being a sort of service department. . . . At any time, more than half the students, especially the [introductory]-level courses, aren't going to be [Star Department] majors." Each of these large courses had a faculty coordinator, and laboratory sections often were filled by teaching assistants or post-docs. While there was some guest lecturing, especially in the graduate courses, in most cases faculty respondents did not indicate that a large degree of functional interaction occurred around teaching responsibilities.

Undergraduate Congruent: Universe Department

In the survey used to select departments, the Universe Department scored as one of the more congruent departments in the university. The mission of the unit intertwined teaching, research, and, as one respondent reported, "an obligation to communicate the excitement of scientific discovery to others." With a great number of instructional and research staff and several large facilities, the Universe Department had a large presence on campus. This stature also is fueled by grant money: the department brought in a great deal of the university's awards. However, this unit has faced a complex series of challenges over the past two decades, mirroring trends in the nationwide disciplinary community. Like the Star Department, the Universe Department also has undergone curricular revisions but was spurred on by very different forces.

In the 1930s, this department was world-renowned. By the 1980s, Associated Research Council rankings placed the program below twentieth among doctoral programs of its type nationwide, while ten of the university's social science and humanities departments ranked in the top ten. In the mid-eighties, a new chair was recruited to improve the prestige of the department. As this chair described in a letter to the college dean, "We are a moderately large, good department that is attempting to become an outstanding department. At least this is how we understand our charge to be—and that is what we want to become. This cannot occur without a surge of new hires."

To increase its status, the department sought to mobilize a number of resources from the university: new faculty lines, equipment, a new building to replace its pre–World War II structure. However, what cost would the department pay for the university's "largesse"? Memos between the chair and the college dean around this period indicate that the college administration sought justification that such staffing could be matched by enrollment, particularly at the undergraduate level. One memo to the dean treated the "concern about the 'small' number of [discipline] majors being trained." (Small is in quotations because the chair disputed the registrar's numbers.) As one full professor pointed out to me and a number of faculty echoed in their comments, "The existence of this department, as big and as well-supported as it is, depends on the teaching load."

However, across the country, the number of majors in this discipline was markedly declining. Nationwide, the percentage of bachelor degrees awarded in the area declined by 75 percent from 1960 to 1996. Even taking this climate into consideration, the department was not among the top twenty-five U.S. departments that awarded BS degrees, an important statistic given the great size of the university in which this unit is located.

The department's responses to these challenges have contributed to its congruence in two significant ways. First, through widespread curricular reforms the department has developed a "universe" of activity around instructional issues. Although estimates of exactly when vary, sometime in the 1990s or early 2000s, the department began to pay more attention to its undergraduate courses. Much of the shift has involved, according to one faculty member, "a number of experiments going on in the department . . . to try to figure out how best to present the materials to the students, how to run the course so the students actually learn, and also how to go about assessing whether or not they are learning."

Several faculty felt that the influx of new faculty that took place during this period was the key factor in changing the department's mission. Ironically, the large number of new hires brought in to increase the department's research prestige instead may have been a major force for instructional change. According to another faculty-administrator, "We have made a number of hires in this department. So we have young people coming in, and they seem to be people who really tend to care about teaching."

Whatever the impetus, by the mid-1990s the department was engaged in a number of experiments and initiatives that focused particularly on reform of introductory courses. A new administrative position had been established to focus on the undergraduate program. The department eliminated some very specialized courses "that were getting enrollments of two students a year" and introduced new courses with a more general focus.

The widespread nature of reforms undertaken during the department's history is significant. Although the reforms are not as visible as those found in other departments across the nation, every respondent told me about their involvement in or knowledge of at least one of the unit's initiatives, often quite proudly. The instructional activity in this department best can be described as like "a universe," where attention to instruction is probably less cutting-edge but more widely dispersed. This explanation aligned with one respondent's hypothesis for the unit's congruence levels: "Anyway, once you begin to implement a new value, then there's a kind of collective effect that takes place that you know your neighbor is worrying more about teaching. So you're inclined to do that [too]."

Overview of Teaching in the Universe Department

The standard load for faculty in the Universe Department is one course (as director) or three sections per term. Much of the department's enrollment is located in large introductory courses, and, accordingly, most of faculty's instructional time is spent in those courses as well. According to the chair, half of the department's "faculty capital" is devoted to staffing the introductory courses. One of the most commented upon features of the instructional structure is faculty-led discussion sections. Professors at all ranks mentioned the uniqueness of this particular arrangement when compared to other departments at this university and at other postsecondary institutions. According to one long-time faculty member, this practice began with very utilitarian motives: a previous chair "figured out that when they're handing out new positions, it's based upon what your credit hours are. He figured out that if he used faculty in recitations, you could have a lot more student credit hours for faculty and could use that to get more positions from the college."

In more contemporary times, the arrangement has been substantiated by claims of pedagogical best practice. As far back as the late 1980s, a visiting committee criticized the department because "the pattern of teaching assignments in the [department] seems unusual to us, in its emphasis on senior faculty teaching of recitation sections on a substantial scale." In a response to the college stimulated by the report, the department responded, "As we have noted in our report on the undergraduate program, the use of faculty to teach recitations has a long tradition in the [Universe] Department, and it brings to our undergraduate students the unique benefits, at an early age in their scientific careers, of contact with senior and experienced scientists." A similar sentiment is expressed by faculty today, one of whom noted, "A lot of other schools have them done by graduate students. We think there's a benefit to additional contact with faculty, in particular those environments where it's more personal."

Graduate Incongruent: Divided Department

Founded more than one hundred years ago, the Divided Department today is a well-respected graduate health science program, among the top quartile in National Research Council (2001) and *Gourman Report* (1997) graduate school rankings. However, in the survey used to select departments, it scored as one of the more incongruent departments in the university.

Departmental records document that there was a significant amount of dissension and conflict over the past decade, much of which reached a level of acrimony that was unusual even for an academic organization. Although never raised by interviewees, three cases of significant dissension over racial and gender bias are noted in university records, involving both intradepartmental tension and conflict between the college and the department. Because these incidents occurred in the mid-1990s, they clearly could have an effect on the department's responses to the 1996 survey used to select this unit. With such tensions and conflict, the potential for divided responses on a range of beliefs about departmental activities is significant.

However, in my interviews, faculty described the current department quite positively, especially noting the chair's effectiveness and support. Although adjectives of this manner could stem from interviewees' desires to self-censor or paint a positive picture of the department, placing the current administration in historical context suggests that this was a comparatively peaceful time in the unit. Because there was a marked shift in descriptions of the unit's climate, a question arises about whether the Divided Department can still be labeled "incongruent." In this chapter, I argue that it can, particularly in the realm of teaching.

Some faculty indicated that the organization's stance toward teaching had changed for the better over the years, which possibly could construct a more congruent instructional climate. For example, one professor felt that the amount of attention devoted to instructional issues had increased: "I think things have changed considerably, in the last fifteen to sixteen years. . . . [It used to be that] really good quality teaching was paid lip service to. . . . And I think that my opinion actually is shared by most other members of the department." Actually, this opinion was not shared by other members. Another respondent felt that teaching was more highly valued by a former college administrative team, and yet another expressed, "I really worry about the teaching aspect of things. Life over here is so focused on success in research." While it is possible that today's faculty body may demonstrate more agreement on other matters of department operations, such as faculty-administrator relationships, it is clear that a marked split remains in beliefs about instructional matters.

Overview of Teaching in the Divided Department

Teaching responsibilities in the Divided Department were split between "service courses," taught to professional, graduate, and undergraduate students outside the department, and graduate instruction, or small seminars or research involving the unit's own doctoral students. Many of the courses in the

Divided Department were taught by multiple instructors. In large service classes, there could be "ten different faculty [who] participate in them."

If the chair was the coach of this departmental group, there were two kinds of players on the team: the "pros," who played high-stakes games that deliver funding and recognition to the group, and the "amateurs," who brought dedication to the basic work needed to keep the team going. In the Divided Department, there was a clear division between graduate instruction, or small seminars and research conducted with the unit's own doctoral students, and service teaching, or large classes taught to professional, graduate, and under-graduate students outside the department. While graduate instruction was highly valued, more appealing to faculty, and often practiced interactively, service teaching was heavily required of the department, yet undervalued, concentrated among a few faculty, and practiced without much communica-tion between instructors.

Graduate Congruent: Team Department

Founded in the late 1980s from a merger of two departments, the Team Department showed the highest level of department-self congruence, both in terms of beliefs about instructional standards and value placed on teaching. Faculty unanimously reported that effective teaching is characteristic of both themselves and of valued colleagues. Additionally, there was a very small mean difference (4 percent) between the time faculty perceived their depart-ment wanted them to spend on teaching and the allocation they preferred.

The unit's name arises from an athletic metaphor named by a respon-dent who was describing faculty dynamics in the department:

> It's kind of a little like managing a soccer team or something. You've got a lot of different personalities and they get in fights once in a while, but you have to be good at managing your own people and understanding them. Getting the most out of them.

The Team Department unit has an influential "coach," or chair, whose cen-trality was shaped by both the historical development of the organization and by personal style.

Like the Divided Department, the Team Department had a conflict-ridden history. Today's Team Department joins two units that originally were distinct. In the late 1980s, the dean decided to group many of the college's departments together to create more efficiencies of scale. Two aca-demic units were merged as part of this reorganization. Because the relation-ship between the heads of the two units was notoriously acrimonious, a new chair was selected for the combined department and "charged with bringing people together." Faculty members present during the transition describe the original interaction between the two units as "good" and "cordial," but with little interaction between faculty in the units. It is astounding that in less than a decade, the department has moved from acrimony to bounded coexistence, to congruence.

Additionally, the department was undergoing another change, or a shift in mission, which also could have been divisive. In the early nineties, the past university president and college dean decided that the college's research base should be increased to improve research funds and institutional prestige. As a result, there was a shift in hiring emphasis, away from clinicians with professional expertise to doctorates with research agendas. In interviews, I paid particular attention to clinical faculty's perspectives to better understand if they felt devalued by this move, but their largely positive views of the department indicated that the mission shift did not have as much impact on congruence as one might expect.

Overview of Teaching in the Team Department

Like the Divided Department, instruction in the Team Department was of a dual nature: courses were offered for both professional students and the unit's own graduate students. Instruction took place in a wide variety of contexts, including patient care, graduate seminars, laboratories, continuing education, and rotating lectures. However, because of the nature of teaching in these contexts and the size of the unit, there was more of an overlap in professorial responsibilities than in the Divided Department.

While the bifurcated character of instructional settings (graduate and service courses) contributed to incongruence in the Divided Department, in the Team Department, the differing structure of these contexts supported a culture of congruence. Why was this the case? Chapters 3 to 5 offer some additional explanation, but one key reason was that many of the larger professional courses were team taught: several faculty supervised students who engaged in patient care or they rotated in their lectures. For example, describing the clinical instructional context, one faculty member reported that "usually, there are two or three faculty members on the floor at a time." Although smaller, the structure of graduate-level courses also facilitated interaction among faculty, as course directors often incorporated guest lectures.

Unlike the other three departments in this study, this congruent department employed a high number of clinical faculty. In contrast to tenured or tenure-track academic faculty, whose responsibilities include a significant research component, clinical faculty were largely devoted to patient care and instruction, in both practice-oriented and didactic settings. Clinical faculty engaged in a tenure-like promotion process, but the qualifications needed for appointment and promotion were less predicated on research accomplishments. While a tenure-track position usually requires the doctorate, clinical appointments more heavily stressed patient experience and some education beyond a professional degree. At the time of this study, clinical, tenured, tenure-track, and emeritus staff in the Team Department numbered greater than fifty; however, only a small fraction of these were full-time academic faculty.

SUMMARY AND CONCLUSIONS

Studies of research university faculty show unique discrepancies between the value they accord to teaching and the worth they perceive their colleagues and administrators assign to the activity. This general pattern may be attributable to the ambiguity associated with instructional goals and objectives in a research university. However, research that focuses only on the institutional level conceals variations in levels of agreement, which differ significantly by department. Here, I examine the particular factors that give rise to differential levels of congruence, or faculty's perception that their beliefs about teaching align with their organization's, among four departments in a single research university.

This book explores how administrative actions and collegial interactions make it possible for colleagues to agree about the value and measurement of effective teaching. Conversely, where such informal networks are weak and policies are ill-communicated, faculty and administrators can hold strong individual opinions about the value of teaching, but their ideas and values seem to exist in isolation.

This work diverges from previous research on congruence levels in several ways. First, although educational literature shows that there can be important variations in levels of agreement about instructional beliefs among faculty by department, it does not precisely specify why these variations occur. Through case studies, this research examines the specific factors that give rise to departments' varying levels of congruence.

Second, it contributes to a body of organizational scholarship, or studies of person-organization fit, by specifying the relationship between organizational structures and congruence levels. Person-organization fit research has a limited view of organizational culture, and I adopt a more intersubjective view that looks beyond formally declared policies to how group members conceptualize and enact their understandings of organizational values in everyday practice.

Finally, the book offers research-based practical strategies for chairs, faculty, future faculty, and faculty developers, or all those in a university who wish to develop a culture of congruence. Most chapters start with a narrative from a popular educational source, such as the *Chronicle of Higher Education*, to illustrate the widespread resonances congruence issues have with faculty life, and they end with practical applications.

CHAPTER TWO

BENEFITS OF INSTRUCTIONAL CONGRUENCE

Outside of Crosley Tower, the University of Cincinnati's campus is coming alive with the start of a new quarter. Inside, the 12th floor feels like a morgue.

The economics department, which occupies the floor, is down to 11 faculty members from the 23 they had a dozen years ago. Graduate students, who used to congregate in a lounge and the hallways outside the chairman's office, haven't been around since 1998, when the department's doctoral program closed.

"The atmosphere here is just deadly," says John A. Powers, an associate professor who has been here for 37 years.

This devastation is the fallout from a war between two faculty groups who clashed over priorities: teaching or research. One side wanted to raise the department in national rankings by focusing on publishing, the other to put a premium on teaching and advising students. (Wilson, 2002)

If you ask a chair, "What are your primary goals for your department?" chances are that "congruence" would not top the list—it would likely be subsumed by tasks such as recruiting faculty and reporting to upper-level administrators (Carroll & Gmelch, 1994). Therefore, this chapter focuses on the benefits of congruence, and the perils of incongruence, for university organizations. Why is the presence of the fit between an individual's own values and perceptions of organizational priorities important? This chapter argues that congruence, or alignment around a consistent set of values around teaching and research, plays a significant role in shaping a department's performance and institutional continuity.

The illustrative case reported above suggests the dangerous effects in-structional incongruence can have on a department. As described in the *Chronicle of Higher Education*, the University of Cincinnati economics de-partment was decimated over faculty's disagreement about the priority that teaching should hold. Such cases may become more common as colleges and universities develop "mission creep," or a shift in institutional orientation toward either a strong research- or teaching-oriented focus, and faculty align themselves with the "new values" or the "old values" (Dubrow, Moseley, & Dustin, 2006). The Cincinnati case suggests that collegial alignment, espe-cially during a change in missions, is fundamental to an organization's long-term survival.

Other scholarship finds that that congruence is associated with in-creased job satisfaction, lower attrition, better job performance, and a strength-ened commitment to the organization (Chatman, 1991; Chatman & Barsade, 1995; Fairweather & Rhoads, 1995; Kristof-Brown, Zimmerman, & Johnson, 2005; Olsen, Maple, & Stage, 1995; O'Reilly, Chatman, & Caldwell, 1991; Peters & Mayfield, 1982; Verquer, Beeher, & Wagner, 2002). However, there is little research about the effect of congruence on job outcomes, or, in the case of faculty, on teaching and student learning. Blackburn and Lawrence (1995) find that faculty who perceive themselves to be at odds with their department or institution's perceived organizational climate spend less time on teaching. This finding is telling, but the authors do not discuss the nature or quality of this teaching, which is significant because less time on teaching does not necessarily equate with "bad teaching" or poor learning outcomes for students (Astin, 1993; Boice, 1991).

In this chapter, I discuss two important relationships that congruence has with the work of teaching. First, I look at the benefits of congruence by examining the difference in student ratings between incongruent and con-gruent departments. Although student ratings are only one measure of in-structional effectiveness, they have been found to correlate with student achievement (such as test scores), as well as peer and expert evaluations of a course (Arreola, 2000; Cashin, 1995). Additionally, because the nature of student assignments and assessments varies immensely by discipline, student ratings are a consistent measure that can be used to highlight potential differences in the learning experience.

Second, I look at the costs of incongruence. I use two case studies to illustrate how instructional misalignment can be detrimental to the department's continuity, both in terms of staffing and also in respect to faculty retention during the tenure and promotion process.

CONGRUENCE AND STUDENT RATINGS

Is departmental congruence associated with more favorable student evaluation of instruction? To explore this question, I compared student ratings for the two large undergraduate science departments, the Star and Universe Departments.

These two high-enrollment units were chosen because many of the courses in the graduate departments enroll few students, and some research on student evaluations indicates that course ratings with fewer than ten students should be interpreted with caution—still others have suggested fifteen as a minimum (Cashin, 1995). Academic discipline can have an effect on student ratings; for example, music courses tend to be rated more highly than engineering courses. However, research shows that the two science disciplines represented here tend not to differ significantly (Cashin, 1990).

For this analysis, student ratings were aggregated for instructors teaching over two years (2004–2005). Two global questions about teaching were used for the analysis:

1. Overall, this was an excellent course
2. Overall, the instructor was an excellent teacher

For each of these questions, students rated their instructors on a five-point scale, with one signifying "strongly disagree" and five meaning "strongly agree."

Analysis based on the four terms included in this study covered all instructors for whom student ratings were reported, including faculty, lecturers, and adjuncts. A quick note on method: Because an instructor who achieves high ratings in one course is likely to receive them in another, an analysis that treats each course's rating as independent would not be appropriate.[8] Results were therefore aggregated by individual instructor. In other words, all of Dr. X's ratings were computed as a weighted mean, which together, served as one data point. Taking into consideration that some instructors may have taught a large number of students while others may have taught a small number of students, each average rating was weighted proportionally to the number of students taught by that instructor. These weights were further normalized by dividing each weight by the average weight to avoid inflating the sample size. Similarly, course structures are related to each other, because a well-organized class one term is likely to be similarly planned the next. Therefore, a second aggregation was done by course number, accompanied by a similar weighting process. Table 4 summarizes the number of instructors and courses that were used for each analysis.

In the congruent Universe Department, instructors taught 336 times during the four terms, which were aggregated for each of the 54 faculty and eight lecturers, and again for the 66 courses. The incongruent Star unit's instructors taught 190 times, and again, these evaluations were averaged for each of the 42 faculty, seven lecturers, and 48 courses in the unit. Independent-sample T-tests were computed for the student evaluation questions pertaining to both the instructor, a reflection of teaching ability, and the course, an indicator of effectiveness of curricular design.

Course level does have one of the most significant impacts on student ratings. Research shows that introductory courses frequently are rated lower, often because they must be taken to meet a requirement or because first- and

Table 4. Levels of Courses and Ranks of Instructors Included in the Student Ratings Comparison

COURSE LEVEL	No. of Unique Courses at Each Level		No. of Unique Tenure-Track Faculty at Each Level†		No. of Unique Lecturers & Adjuncts at Each Level†	
	Congruent Dept.	Incongruent Dept.	Congruent Dept.	Incongruent Dept.	Congruent Dept.	Incongruent Dept.
Introductory (0–199; some 200-level)	11	7	27	9	6	4
Intermediate (200-499)	28	20	36	34	5	4
Advanced (500+)	27	21	22	20	0	0
No. Unique Courses/Instructors	66	48	54	42	8	7

†Many instructors taught over multiple levels, so the totals of these columns will be greater than the number of unique instructors in each department.

second-year students tend to rate less highly (Arreola, 2000; Feldman, 1979). Therefore, it is important to address course level when comparing student ratings between the departments. A department with a greater proportion of introductory courses, or instructors teaching those classes, might see lower ratings as a result of this arrangement.

Distribution of Teaching Work

As Table 4 illustrates, teaching work is organized quite differently in the congruent and incongruent undergraduate science departments. One striking difference is the distribution in the types of courses faculty teach. Distinctions are particularly notable in the introductory course, the gateway to a science major or premedical concentration. To illustrate, only a minority (21%) of faculty in the Star Department who taught during the four terms were ever instructors for a 100-level course. In contrast, half (50%) of the Universe Department's faculty taught a gateway course.

One obvious reason for this difference is that the Universe Department offered nearly double the number of introductory courses, when compared to Star Department offerings. However, taking a historical viewpoint, the large number of both introductory course offerings and faculty who teach in them are a legacy of the department making an organizational decision to increase the proportion of faculty who teach in these classes, as described in chapter 1.

Ratings by Course Level

When comparing course ratings, the higher student ratings for the congruent departments are noteworthy. On a scale of one to five, with higher scores indicating a more favorable evaluation, the Universe Department's courses were given an average student rating of 3.9, while the Star Department's gateway classes were evaluated with a 3.7 average (Table 5). This mean difference of 0.2 was statistically significant (p<.001). It is also interesting to note the lower standard deviation, or spread, of course ratings in the Universe Department, suggesting that there is more uniformity in course performance, such as one would expect in a congruent unit.

There is also a gap in student ratings of their instructors: Universe staff received a mean evaluation of 4.2, whle Star instructors scored 4.0. However, this mean difference of 0.2 is only marginally significant (p<.10).

Of course, the findings presented here are trends, and an individual course or instructor in the incongruent department could score more highly than one in the congruent unit. However, the ratings presented here suggest that there are notable benefits for the congruent department, at least in the eyes of students.

Table 5. Comparison of Student Ratings of Instructors and Courses by Department

	Course Ratings			Instructor Ratings		
	Congruent Dept. Standardized Weighted Mean (SD)	Incongruent Dept. Standardized Weighted Mean (SD)	Mean Difference	Congruent Dept. Standardized Weighted Mean (SD)	Incongruent Dept. Standardized Weighted Mean (SD)	Mean Difference
	3.9 (0.25) n=66	3.7 (0.48) n=48	0.2 **	4.2 (0.48) n=62	4.0 (0.68) n=49	0.2 *

*p<.10; **p<.001

Discussion of Findings

Even considering that a greater proportion of the congruent department's offerings were concentrated in the introductory levels, it still saw higher student ratings. However, it is important to highlight that the distinctions among faculty evaluations were more pronounced in the course ratings.

Given that congruence is an organizational characteristic, it is not surprising that most of its benefits appear in the organizational dimension of ratings. Course designs are highly influenced by structural factors, such as curricular arrangements, attrition patterns, and ways that committees are able to reflect on and design an effective learning environment. Courses often are products that result both from an individual instructor's contribution to a syllabus and departmental discussion and feedback on the course plan.

Additionally, here, the organization of teaching work may have a large impact on the ratings, as the Universe Department employed a lesser proportion of lecturers in its introductory courses. Feldman's literature review (1983) finds that while the majority of studies on the effect of rank on teaching evaluations show no significant relationship, those that do establish a connection indicate that rank is positively associated with students' overall evaluations of the instructor and the class.

The fact that the congruent department can focus more of its own resources on introductory courses and still see ratings gains should not be downplayed, especially given the disciplines in which these departments are located. Attrition from the sciences has been spotlighted as a national problem, and the first two years of college have a significant impact on students' decisions to leave (Committee on Science, Engineering, and Public Policy, 2006; Manis, Thomas, Sloat, & Davis, 1989; Seymour & Hewitt, 1997). The introductory, or gateway, course has been targeted as one important influence in student attrition, as even talented students can quickly be turned off to the discipline (Tobias, 1990). Additionally, because of their larger size and the diversity of students in an introductory course, it can be extraordinarily challenging to teach these courses well.

It is important to highlight that the relationship between congruence and student ratings is not causal. Indeed, as later chapters will show, the relationship is most definitely an association: factors that are related to congruence (such as well-thought-out systems of team teaching) will most likely also be more effective teaching practices that will be reflected in higher student evaluations. However, it is telling that there is a statistically significant association between congruence and student ratings, which could have a great impact on undergraduates.

INSTITUTIONAL CONTINUITY

The previous section used a statistical analysis to highlight student ratings differences between the Universe and Star Departments. I now shift gears methodologically and substantively to describe how incongruence also may have an impact on another dimension of organizational performance, or institutional continuity.

Both incongruent departments had cultures in which there were clear divisions in faculty's beliefs about teaching. Faculty indicated that there was much ambiguity about how to assess teaching in the department and dissensus about how instructional work is valued. The resulting problems of this congruence are similar for both units. First, faculty who are heading toward an evaluation—whether for promotion, tenure, or merit pay—may find it hard to understand and reconcile personal goals and perceived administrative priorities. Second, questions of institutional continuity were raised for both departments. Because each unit possesses a key powerful actor in each unit around instructional issues, the operation of the department may be compromised when these people leave.

Divided Department

In the case of the incongruent graduate department, the Divided Department, there was an interesting split between the value accorded to teaching graduate students in the department and the worth given to teaching "service courses," or large courses that often met other departments' curricular requirements. By all accounts, faculty valued the teaching of their doctoral students, and the chair exerted a strong pressure for faculty to devote sufficient time and energy to teaching. However, there was a perceived opportunity cost to service classes, especially if one were the course director, the faculty member with responsibility for coordinating the class's lectures, assessments, and logistics. Because they are large, didactic, and general, time devoted to managing the course was time that could have been spent on research.

One faculty member who taught a good proportion of the service courses described this personal opportunity cost in conversations with the chair: "I think [the chair] realizes that I do a good job [at teaching]. I think [the chair] realizes that I do a lot . . . but, there is a written requirement that you are supposed to bring in [a good proportion of] your own salary from grants, and every year [the chair] has said, 'We are going to have to cut you back. I will try to find ways to cover that [proportion], but I just want to let you know that it is coming.' So I may wind up taking a salary cut." The decision to teach service courses held implications not only for one's career and salary but also for the department, which used external funding to free up general funds for expenses such as faculty raises.

As a result of the personal and organizational costs, only a few people took responsibility for much of the didactic teaching, and they were disproportionately senior faculty. This arrangement was recognized as a potential trouble spot, for these professors' impending retirements foreshadowed an instructional void. One respondent told me, "When they retire, we are all in trouble." As a result, there is a conflict: although higher level administrators require the department to teach several service courses, faculty think they do not value this activity because it does not bring in grant dollars. In consequence, there are only a few senior faculty who are willing to take on these duties. A faculty-administrator commented on this dynamic: "I have become aware of the concern that the faculty have that we seem to be getting two classes of faculty, the ones that teach graduate students and the ones that do service classes. And there seems to be a sense at the level of the junior faculty that they do not want to teach service courses. They want to teach graduate courses. And frankly I have to deal with that."

The department's culture of incongruence has profound implications for its operations, especially in the long term. One result of its incongruence is that a potential crisis looms in the department's future. Soon, faculty who take significant responsibility for the service courses will retire, as could the chair, raising the question of institutional continuity. Who will take on these instructional positions, given the opportunity costs for doing so? If the current chair leaves or retires, will the next head be as concerned with or involved in instructional decisions?

Star Department

Like the previous unit, a lot of the Star Department's activities around pedagogy were associated with one faculty member. Earlier, I described this person as a star, but in an interview, the respondent used another similar metaphor to describe himself: "I am the little island in [the discipline] at the [University]." Indeed, this "island" has been quite successful in gaining recognition for curricular reforms and increasing the department's enrollment. However, like the first case presented, there are two difficulties with this institutional arrangement. First, if the "island" leaves, what then? Without an understudy waiting in the wings, there will be an instructional leadership void.

Second, this concentration of information about instructional matters becomes problematic for faculty because they have less access to data about standards for effective teaching and the value colleagues place on teaching. Other mentors, who could have been the vehicle for communicating administrative instructional expectations, instead seem to emphasize research responsibilities, because that is what is most prized by the department. (Rohrer [1997] also reports that new faculty mentors often do not convey messages about institutional policy, especially around teaching.) For example, tenured faculty and chairs indicated that while they generally valued instructional efforts, they did not encourage junior faculty to spend a lot of time on teaching. These messages also were described by one assistant professor: "I also know that people may overemphasize to new faculty members that they shouldn't spend too much time on teaching because newer faculty members tend to spend too much time on teaching. . . . If that is why they say that to

junior faculty all of the time it is because they know how easy it is to get
sucked into spending all of your time in doing a top-notch job. Maybe they
actually value teaching more than I think they do."

Junior faculty noted that this emphasis on research seemed somewhat
at odds with college-level messages that teaching plays a significant role in
the tenure process. For example, one assistant professor noted that "in [this
department], the [tenure] emphasis is definitely not on teaching," yet at the
college's orientation, "there, the emphasis is on teaching." Because of these
divisions, junior faculty indicate that there is much dissensus or ambiguity
about important issues such as who is "allowed" to devote a good deal of time
to instruction, what constitutes instructional standards, and what makes for
a valued faculty member.

Impact on Junior Faculty

While the previous sections focused on the potential impact of incongruence
for organizational continuity in general, incongruence may have a particularly influential effect on junior faculty. Ambiguity for junior faculty about
how to be an "effective teacher" could prove problematic, especially if they
do not feel they have the clarity of information needed to enact the teaching
standards in tenure and promotion. Additionally, congruence may also play
a direct part in the tenure and promotion process, such as in the Divided
Department. Both faculty and chairs throughout the Divided Department's
college indicated in another interview study that it was somewhat desirable
for those up for promotion to "profess congruence with departmental goals
and norms." If congruence does figure into in the review process, this
department's faculty may be disadvantaged compared to tenure candidates in
other units.

Of the seven junior faculty [9] in incongruent departments, nearly all
explained the misalignment of the self-colleague measures of effective teaching by pointing to the ambiguity and hidden nature of instructional standards. Many felt that they did not know how "effective teaching" was
operationalized in the department. For example, one asked semi-rhetorically,
"How do you know [if colleagues are effective teachers]?" I questioned back,
"How do *you* know if you are an effective teacher?" "I don't know," replied
this respondent. Another offered, "I don't know which of my colleagues are
effective teachers and which are not. In fact, I bet my colleagues don't know
either." Others thought that measures existed in the department, but that
each person had a different understanding of effective teaching.

Given that research plays the main role in all of these departments'
tenure and promotion equations, this may not have an impact. Admittedly,
it is too early to tell, as some of the respondents have not yet gone up for
tenure. To illustrate the difficulty of comparisons, in both the Star and
Universe Departments, two-thirds of the respondents who were up for tenure

in each unit did get promoted. However, half of the respondents in the Star Department are still awaiting review, while all of the Universe Department interviewees have been through the process. (All candidates for tenure in both graduate departments were successful, but again, some are awaiting review.)

However, other research suggests that in research universities, faculty's stress about both teaching and formal review increases the longer they work at the institution, and those who leave are more likely to give lower ratings to their institution's support system for teaching than do those who stay (Bechhofer & Barnhart, 1999; Menges, 1999). Therefore, congruent cultures simply may offer a better work climate for new faculty, even if the environment does not carry implications for tenure and promotion decisions.

CONCLUSION

The concept of congruence shares many features of Senge's (1990, 2000) "learning organizations," where members are connected to an institution's mission, goals, opportunities, and problems. Senge finds that learning organizations are higher performing and better able to adapt to changing environments because they understand complexity, share a vision for the organization with others, work as a team, and support individual growth. Therefore, it is not surprising that the findings on congruence presented here and elsewhere suggests that alignment is associated with job performance, institutional continuity, and job satisfaction.

How can departments achieve congruence in order to reap these benefits? Kezar (2005, p. 52) describes the university as "institutional structures and cultures that reify and reinforce individualistic work," and as discussed in the previous chapter, these organizational features tend to create incongruent environments around teaching. However, chapter 3 examines how certain policies and practices that focus on the evaluation of teaching can overcome these institutional barriers. Similarly, chapter 4 turns to instructional structures that help promote teaching networks, and these, too, can help to construct a culture of congruence.

CHAPTER THREE

"IT'S LIKE BAD TASTE": HOW INTERPRETIVE
STRUCTURES CONTRIBUTE TO
PERSON-ORGANIZATION FIT

A recent cartoon depicts a very long and complicated equation written on a large blackboard. A bedraggled professor has just reached the end of the equation and writes, "TENURE" in large letters (Thaves, 2004). One possible interpretation of this picture is that the professor has just solved such a valuable equation that he has unlocked the key to tenure. However, for an assistant professor working in a research university, the cartoon may take on another meaning: tenure as a near-impossible to understand process. In a research university, teaching standards can make this process even more opaque, as they often are not clearly defined by departments nor well understood by faculty.

In this chapter, I begin with a discussion of the literature on person-organization fit in order to understand how others have explained congruence. I then discuss how my approach to congruence differs from established person-organization fit research. I focus primarily on how faculty make meaning of formal policy, as well as what department practices can facilitate the

Frank and Ernest

development of clear understandings. However, this research is not dismissive of formal policies around teaching, such as guidelines for peer review and student ratings. Instead, I find that formal guidelines on teaching can be most effective if they facilitate the process of social interpretation of the policy; that is, if the policy itself encourages interaction around instructional matters, especially between administrators and faculty.

PERSON-ORGANIZATION FIT

The alignment of a faculty member's teaching beliefs with those of departmental colleagues, chairs, deans, and central administrators represents an example of "person-organization fit."[10] Defined as "the congruence between the norms and values of organizations and the values of persons," studies of person-organization fit can be grouped into two categories (Chatman, 1989, p. 339).

The first classification uses measures of congruence that match an individual's values and a researcher's measure of organizational culture. Studies of this type compare individual beliefs and peers' understandings of climate (Ostroff & Rothausen, 1997), values reported by organizational members presumed to be more knowledgeable about the organization by virtue of their tenure or position (Chatman, 1989, 1991; O'Reilly, Chatman, & Caldwell, 1991), and experimentally constructed work simulations embodying a particular ethic, such as collectivity (Chatman & Barsade, 1995). A second group of research looks at subjectively measured congruence, or an individual's perception that her beliefs and goals align with the organization (Olsen, Maple, & Stage, 1995; O'Reilly & Chatman, 1986; Verquer, Beehr, & Wagner, 2002).

Both bodies of person-organization fit research find that organizational structure plays a significant role in facilitating congruence (Chatman, 1989, 1991; Chatman & Barsade, 1995; O'Reilly, Chatman, & Caldwell, 1991; Ostroff & Rothausen, 1997). For example, formally organized practices, such as mentoring programs and spending time with newcomers before they enter an organization, are seen as determinants of alignment (Chatman, 1991).

Interestingly, a parallel argument frequently is made in the educational literature, although the organizational structures discussed here are extrinsic rewards in tenure and promotion policies (Boyer, 1990; Clark, 1987; Cuban, 1999; Hutchings & Shulman, 1999; Sykes, 1988). Although the context for these accounts differ, all essentially argue that research university faculty's interests in good teaching are defeated by reward structures that punish faculty who spend a significant amount of time away from research. Presumably, if all faculty were offered formal incentives to influence faculty to value teaching, there also would be more person-organization fit around instructional beliefs.

However, both of these literatures give only cursory attention to how the process of subjective verification occurs, or how policies are actually understood and interpreted. This omission most likely follows from their lack of focus on the intersubjective nature of organizational beliefs. Fit researchers themselves, Kristof-Brown, Zimmerman, and Johnson (2005, p. 41) write, "Specifically, a better understanding of what it means to people to 'fit' and the mechanisms that stimulate fit are long overdue." While person-organization fit literature finds that some structures are associated with congruence, it does not specify how they facilitate alignment of beliefs among organizational members. These dynamics can be explored by examining not only the nature and intention of organizational structures (e.g., department workshops to engage all faculty in discussions of new instructional techniques) but also their actual effects (e.g., perhaps few faculty actually attend such events). Likewise, there may be a more complex relationship between extrinsic rewards and faculty's beliefs and behaviors around teaching, because faculty may not know about, understand, or value the instructional incentives offered to them (Astin, Korn, & Dey, 1991; Colbeck, 1994; O'Meara, 2003). Sewell (1992, p. 19) describes this process as the "polysemy of resources," or how resources carry many meanings that can be interpreted uniquely by different actors.

A fuller understanding of organizational culture as "grounded in the shared assumptions of individuals participating in organizations" emphasizes the degree to which the presence of centrally declared missions, policies, and values cannot fully explain the presence of congruence (Tierney, 1988, p. 4).[11] To capture this intersubjective nature of organizational beliefs, I henceforth use the term *culture of congruence*, rather than "person-organization fit," to indicate alignment of beliefs.

A clear example of the difference between formal policy and clarity of interpretation can be found in student evaluations. Widely used throughout U.S. colleges and universities, an extensive body of research has found student evaluations to be reliable and valid measures of effective teaching (Arreola, 2000; Marsh, 1987; Marsh & Roche, 1997). However, many instructors or chairs personally do not find them to be credible, and the popular and scholarly literature offers three main critiques of their use.

First, many find that student ratings are simply a measure of how easy or entertaining a course is (Aleamoni, 1987; Ory, 2001). The following quote, from a highly read educational publication, illustrates this common perspective:

> The message is clear: "Teach us less; require less." On the bright side, no instructor need fear students or administrators showing up at the office demanding harder courses, more demanding workloads, and stricter grading. Professors who want to raise evaluation scores can do so quite easily by simply complying with student demands and dumbing down their courses. . . . It is hard to imagine a practice more harmful to higher education than one that encourages instructors to satisfy the demands and pleas of students who resent the

appropriate rigors of college instruction. These forms are not just invalid and unreliable; they are pernicious. (Trout, 1997, p. 24)

A second key critique, which is still hotly debated in the literature, is that some ratings reflect student stereotypes and therefore discriminate against certain groups of faculty, particularly women and minorities (Basow, 1998; Feldman, 1992; Feldman, 1993; Kardia & Wright, 2004). Finally, research on how student evaluations are utilized notes that chairs and administrators may utilize student evaluations for faculty performance evaluations, but not fully understand their applications (Franklin & Theall, 1990).

Whether these are valid critiques of student ratings lies outside the scope of this book. However, they are key examples of the dismissal of one very common method of teaching evaluation, despite an extensive research and administrative backing. Although these are very different critiques of the use of student ratings for the evaluation of instruction, they share a common implication. To be more useful, both instructors and administrators need to develop shared understandings about useful tools for evaluating teaching in their own classrooms, whether it is student ratings or another measure. These shared understandings provide the foundation for interpretive structures, which are discussed in the following section.

INTERPRETIVE STRUCTURES

Instead of focusing singularly on formal organizational structures (e.g., tenure policies, leadership, instructional programs) and their impact on congruence, this book explores *interpretive structures*, or shared guidelines for everyday practice. Because they can be interpreted in many different ways, formal institutional policies and practices must be translated by faculty into meaningful standards that can be used systematically to judge others' instructional values and behaviors. Formal policy may govern high-stakes personnel decisions, but interpretive structures establish the rules by which faculty evaluate themselves and each other on a daily basis.

The ambiguous nature of teaching in the research university environment establishes the conditions for the development of various sense-making processes, in which faculty may develop highly elaborate explanations to explain how "the system" works (Louis, 1980; March, 1982; March & Olsen, 1976; O'Meara, 2003; Weick, 1979a, 1979b, 1995). All faculty develop interpretations of a policy, attributing their own meaning to it. However, not all faculty develop interpretive *structures*, as these exist only when there is a patterned, or shared, nature of those interpretations that allow faculty and chairs to put policy into practice. (This use of structure relies upon Sewell's [1992, p. 19] framework, where structures are "sets of mutually sustaining schemas and resources that empower and constrain social action and that tend to be reproduced by that social action.") Without interpretive structures, faculty have few means of ascertaining their colleagues' and chairs' stances on instruction.

The following conversation illustrates the difference between interpretation and interpretive structures. In one of my interviews, I asked a faculty member in an incongruent department how someone could get tenure. Promisingly, he began the response by enumerating five specific formal guidelines for tenure, including doing a "decent" job at teaching. I began to think that this faculty member had a lot of clarity about the process of tenure. However, when I asked him what it meant specifically to be a "decent teacher," I saw that my initial reaction was off base. When it came to putting the formal instructional measures into practice, the respondent thought that each department member had a unique understanding of effective teaching. "Everyone's standard is so different," he told me. Without this clarity about what formal policies mean for everyday practice, alignment of beliefs among faculty is unlikely.

Each member of a department does not need to have an identical interpretation of how to operationalize "effective teaching," but faculty in congruent departments will have a repertoire of understandings about how to put formal policy into systematic practice. Without this translation, faculty can report that they are knowledgeable about formal policies, but that they have little clarity about how they impact actual instructional practice.

Some faculty may resist the development of shared interpretive structures because they feel that good teaching "is so singular an art that it defies definition" (Seldin, 1990, p. 6). Through lack of interaction with colleagues or administrators, others simply may be unaware of what the formal policies are or how fellow department members put them into practice. Still others may reject all formal mechanisms yet substitute evaluative systems that cannot be shared, being reliant on personal intuition. However, development of shared interpretive structures facilitates the development of a congruent teaching culture.

This is not to say that formal policy does not matter. Without the presence of teaching policies, there would be no baseline for faculty to develop their interpretations about the worth of the activity. However, my argument does imply that formal policies must encourage or be accompanied by processes that encourage faculty to understand and make sense of the policy for their daily practice.

The Development of Interpretive Structures

In this study, the perception of the weight accorded to teaching in the reward system was essentially constant. In other words, all faculty felt that the university prioritized research over teaching and service when it came to promotion and tenure. While there was some variation in how teaching effectiveness was measured, the most striking distinction between faculty in incongruent and congruent departments was how they were able to instantiate formal policy, or construct shared interpretive structures around instruction.

Graduate Departments

The departments that focused on graduate teaching (the Team and Divided Departments) showed significant differences in faculty's interpretations of how teaching should be weighted and measured. To formally judge effective teaching for tenure and promotion decisions in the incongruent Divided Department, the chair relied upon written student comments, how much teaching was done, and his firsthand knowledge of the quality of teaching, based on short classroom visitations. From the faculty perspective, respondents also mentioned student ratings and observations, but they spoke also of two different mechanisms by which they might evaluate effective teaching: graduate student performance and subject matter knowledge.

However, faculty had difficulties with the utilization of each of these measurement tools. For example, graduate student performance could not be objectively defined, disciplinary knowledge was hard to assess in a highly interdisciplinary department, and student ratings were not seen as valid. The following is a sampling of Divided Department faculty's thoughts on student evaluations:

- "destructive"

- "wrong"

- students are "fooled" by entertaining, yet unsubstantive, lectures

- qualitative comments indicate that students are authors of "very strange things"

All evaluation measures were found to have flaws, and as a result a fifth mechanism was raised: personal intuition. In fact, intuition was seen the most valuable way of determining who was effective. The following dialogue illustrates this phenomenon, as the respondent subsequently mentions, then rejects, a number of observable mechanisms by which effective teaching could be measured in the unit, coming out in favor of an "intuitive" decision:

R: You get student evaluations, and they go a long way in telling you if you're doing an effective job. But, sometimes students can be wrong. [In addition, t]ypically, what often happens is that people audit classes. . . . But it's very difficult. It's not like taking an exam. But I think that, particularly if you co-direct a course, and you have a colleague with you, you know whether the course has been a success. . . . But there's nothing really objective. But I tell you this, if you ask faculty in our department, "Who are the good lecturers?" they know who the good lecturers are. If you go and ask our graduate students, they'll go tell you who the good lecturers are. The lecturers who put the time, in terms of the preparation and delivery of the material.

MW: So is it that you know it when you see it [laughs]?

R: Yes. It's like bad taste. Or good taste [laughs].

These idiosyncratic understandings of effective teaching, which could vary from person to person, supported a lack of congruence in the department.

In contrast, faculty in the congruent Team Department were asked to compile teaching portfolios for formal evaluations, which included student evaluations, peer evaluations, and metrics for student performance. Faculty in the department validated several mechanisms to ascertain who was an effective teacher, many of which overlapped with formal policies for making such determinations.

For example, faculty indicated that the department's practice of circulating student evaluations opened a window into others' classrooms. In other departments, individuals could assess their own teaching through the use of student ratings; in this unit, faculty had a mechanism for evaluating their colleagues', as well as the entire organization's, instructional effectiveness. Additionally, the unit had a well-established, yet informal, system for observing others' classrooms. Because teaching was heavily structured around sequential courses, overlapping instructors, and team-teaching, it was possible for all faculty to be effective observers nearly all of the time; they could gather information about what others were doing in the classroom. One respondent described how sitting in on her colleagues' courses informed her that many different types of pedagogy could be effective: "I think that they are very different teaching styles, but I think they probably are all very effective at confirming the information in a useful way to the students."

The Team Department had a repertoire of practices—student comments, peer feedback, and student outcomes—to informally and formally assess teaching. Although faculty taught in many different ways, these practices allowed Team Department faculty to construct shared interpretive structures, so that professors could evaluate colleagues' instructional effectiveness and administrators' views on teaching.

Undergraduate Departments

Both of the departments that emphasized undergraduate instruction (the Star and Universe Departments) utilized similar formal standards for determining "excellent" teaching performance in promotion and tenure procedures. However, the way faculty in congruent and incongruent departments developed interpretive structures to operationalize these standards differed significantly.

In the incongruent undergraduate unit, the Star Department, administrators indicated that effective teaching formally was ascertained by a professor's student evaluations (especially outliers), the instructor's absenteeism record, and written complaints from students, if applicable. For promotion and tenure, a faculty member's efforts and accomplishments in developing and revising new courses also would be considered. From the faculty perspective, the three instructional assessments mentioned by respondents were peer review, student ratings, and informal feedback from colleagues and students. However, the first two sources of data were heavily criticized by faculty: peer review was inconsistently and inefficiently administered, while student ratings were not perceived to be a valid measure of one's teaching effectiveness. The problem then becomes, as one Star Department professor stated, "If you can't trust the students and you can't trust the faculty . . . then [teaching is] a difficult thing to quantify."

Without official, credible mechanisms to evaluate teaching, faculty assigned heightened weight to informal and unstructured feedback gleaned from interactions with other faculty and students. For example, the faculty member quoted above felt that her/his colleagues' definition of effective teaching reflected judgments of who was "nice." Another respondent emphasized the intuitive mechanisms needed to learn about what a "reasonable job of teaching" means: "It's unclear to me [laughs]. I guess it means don't get bad evaluations. Or maybe get bad evaluations once, but never again. . . . No one has ever really [directly told me]—it's all just suggested." The most valued feedback was the most individualized and unsystematic, relying upon comments heard from peers or students. Consequently, although it was clear that faculty had developed their own personal interpretations of how to evaluate teaching, there was little indication that they had developed shared interpretive structures that followed from formal policies and practices.

In the congruent undergraduate unit, the Universe Department, administrators described many of the same mechanisms by which they evaluated teaching: student evaluations, peer review, consideration of course context factors (such as the stringency of course expectations), and curricular work (e.g., having a taught a large introductory course, major contributions to major or course development, or instructional innovation). Faculty also identified two of these summative tools: most frequently student ratings, but also general instructional involvement.

Like members of the incongruent undergraduate department, respondents expressed some skepticism about the validity of ratings to measure effective teaching. Faced with this questionable regard for ratings, faculty might have reacted like those in the incongruent department, where faculty experienced a void about how else to evaluate instruction. However, they offered three reasons, cultural and structural, for why members of their department held congruent beliefs. First, the department was experiencing a rise in student ratings, and so many felt that students might be able to appreciate tough, yet effective, instructional approaches.

Second, beliefs about student ratings were intertwined with beliefs about working and teaching in the discipline. One faculty-administrator indicated that compared to other departments, they got lower student ratings, but felt that this dynamic did not discourage faculty because of the impact of collective experience.

> We've also been through it. We've all been through this as students. We all made the choice to go into [discipline], which means that we will take challenging classes our whole academic career and that our grade point averages would not be all that great compared to other students who did otherwise. But it's because we loved [the discipline], and we just think it's great. And so, you know, that's the price you pay. You have to work very hard. And with not much reward.

As a result, the shared experience of "making it" in the profession allowed faculty to develop a sense of confidence in colleagues' abilities, that faculty could be effective teachers, even if their ratings were perceived to be temporarily low.

Third, and most importantly, even those faculty who dismissed student ratings suggested other ways that they operationalized the department's instructional standards. For example, multiple respondents mentioned that a diagnostic exam given to students before and at the end of the semester provided information about the effectiveness of an instructor and offered a department-level understanding of student learning. Like administrators, others thought that involvement in activities such as teaching innovations, instructional grants, a seminar series aimed at lay people from the community, and instruction at a variety of course levels would "count" toward measurement of their teaching record. Finally, because so many of the faculty taught introductory courses, faculty felt that they had a shared sense of how teaching should be done and what outcomes should be expected. One respondent noted, "All of us are sort of in the same boat with a certain level of teaching."

Interestingly, many of the tools mentioned by Universe Department respondents varied, so that one group of faculty mentioned one mechanism and several other respondents highlighted another. In other words, the department did not have an interpretive mechanism that was used by all faculty, such as the Team Department possessed, which might be attributable to the larger size of the Universe Department.[12] However, Universe faculty had developed locally validated tools that were shared by multiple colleagues, in order to create a repertoire of understandings about effective teaching. These understandings about what constitutes effective instruction offered benchmarks for faculty to make their assessments of colleagues' abilities.

FORMAL POLICIES THAT *DO* MATTER

Thus far, I have prioritized how faculty *understand* instructional polices procedures over the *content* of those formal procedures. The reason for this focus
is that faculty's interpretation of official policy has frequently been overlooked in the literatures on person-organization fit and rewards for teaching.
However, the content of the policy, particularly how it encourages social
interaction about the definition of teaching expectations, can play a significant
role in facilitating faculty's understanding of the document.

Team Department

The procedure for tenure and promotion in the congruent graduate department is very similar to the other units in this study. First, a tenure committee
makes recommendations to the chair. Second, the chair submits a recom-
mendation to the college's appointments, promotions, and tenure committee. Third, the college's dean and executive committee use this report to
make a tenure decision; and finally, this decision is submitted to the university's
provost and board. (Clinical faculty participated in an identical process,
except that they were not required to submit external reviews.) Also similar
to the other departments are the areas in which faculty were evaluated:
teaching, scholarly activity, and service (which, in the case of the Team
Department, includes patient care).

However, for the Team Department's college, the guidelines for such
decisions were specified in much more detail, especially for teaching expectations. The formal college document that outlines appointment, promotions, and tenure standards began generally with a statement that teaching
effectiveness was judged by instructional quality, innovation, student impact,
and level of instructional responsibility, as measured by peer and chair evaluations, as well as student and documentary sources. Over the next two pages
(more space than it devoted to scholarly activity), the resource gave specific
indicators of these criteria (e.g., development of new courses as a measure of
"innovation") and how to document them.

Because so many standards for teaching in the research university are
unstated, this college's tenure and promotion document was unique in detail-
ing so extensively the procedure for evaluation of teaching. As understanding is a necessary condition for agreement, transparency of procedures around
teaching helps to construct a sense of congruence between individuals and
decision makers.

However, perhaps more important is the way that these policies can
cultivate social interaction around teaching, which can facilitate the development of interpretive structures. In its call for "input into the evaluation
from peers, departmental chairpersons, students, and other sources," this policy

encourages administrators and colleagues to more frequently observe and discuss each other's teaching.

On the department level as well, the Team Department enacted a number of formal practices to further clarify faculty's understandings of effective teaching and the value accorded to instruction by the organization. It was the only unit to publicly circulate student comments, and such a collective review process can make clear a department's teaching expectations (Cuban, 1999).

Universe Department

Faculty-administrators in the Universe Department described the tenure process as an annual merit review writ large, noting a 50 percent:30 percent:20 percent (research: teaching: service) weighting system that was carried over to the tenure decision:

> My understanding of the university policy is that to get tenure at this university, they don't give you a numerical sort necessarily, but they weigh your research efforts by 50 percent, your teaching efforts by 30 percent, and your service contributions by 20 percent. Now for assistant professors going up for tenure, they don't worry about the service so much. But what our department does is we keep those weights, and we rank everybody every year within each of those categories, and then your merit raise is determined on the basis of those weights. Then after six years time, when you come up for tenure, your tenure case, your promotion case is written. My understanding is that [the college] basically applies the same weights to the stuff that you write in that promotion case and give to them. So that's how teaching figures into it. If you want to think of it this way, the way we do merit raises is sort of a miniature tenure review every year. Because it's in the same spirit with the same weights, and the same positive aspects that will get you tenure, will get you a higher merit raise. Right. So, there's a little bit of consistency there.

The 30 percent allocated to instruction was assessed through student ratings scores (contextualized by written comments), as well as peer reviews by faculty-administrators, personnel committee members, and mentors; and curricular efforts. This consistency offered a common language for discussing tenure, and I frequently heard faculty reference the "50:30:20 formula."

Additionally, out of the four departments in this study, faculty in the congruent undergraduate named probably the most "objective" means of gathering data about teaching and learning, the use of a longitudinal system for collecting course-wide student scores on diagnostic tests. An exam given to students before and at the end of the semester provides information about both the effectiveness of an instructor and a department-level understanding of student learning. Because several faculty utilized this measure, the process of comparing results about student performance encouraged social interaction around instruction in this department.

CONCLUSION

Person-organization fit research usefully establishes that formal policies matter—without them, faculty would have no reference point from which to construct interpretive structures. However, formal policies are only one of the organizational features needed for faculty to gain an understanding of their department's instructional values. In order for faculty to learn about these organizational guidelines, they need to be disseminated and discussed by administrators and by other faculty. If there is limited interaction between faculty and administrative representatives—the chair, assistant chairs, personnel committee members—it is difficult for a faculty member to be cognizant of both formal instructional standards and how they are understood by an academic unit's administrators.

As suggested by person-organization fit literature, the degree of administrative-faculty interaction can be influenced by organizational structures. However, I argue that person-organization fit research needs to take a more intersubjective view of organizational culture, one that depends not only on formal policies and stances, but also on how they are understood and enacted by organizational members. While person-organization fit literature statistically correlates some formal organizational structures with agreement, it gives only cursory attention to *how* alignment occurs. With a more intersubjective perspective, we can better examine how the way that chairs and administrative proxies promote interaction with faculty around discussion of policies enables members to translate them into collective practice. This development of interpretive structures is necessary for a culture of congruence to flourish.

What are the practical implications for ways to document and evaluate teaching effectiveness? First, recent educational movements have focused on changing the rewards structure at research universities. However, there has been less emphasis on the transparency of and constructed meanings arising from existing personnel evaluation mechanisms. I would suggest that considerations about the *quantity* of awards allocated to teaching should be matched with attention given to the *clarity* of these policies.

Second, student evaluations are one of the most common means of measuring teaching effectiveness. However, based on accounts presented here and elsewhere (Franklin & Theall, 1990; Ory, 2001), many faculty appear to have an extraordinarily fraught relationship with student ratings, so much so that it will be near-impossible for administrators to encourage productive discussions (or interpretive structures) with this tool in mind.

Much research on the evaluation of teaching suggests multiple measures (e.g., Arreola, 2000), which allow faculty and administrators to add to their toolbox mechanisms that best fit a department's culture and are accepted as valid measures of effective teaching by faculty. If faculty in a department historically have had an antagonistic relationship with student ratings, administrators may need to consider other means of evaluating teaching that are more palatable to the organization or ways of reframing the use of course evaluations.

Some examples of more culturally acceptable ways of measuring teaching that were presented here are measurement of student gains in a course through diagnostic tests or presentation of a professional development narrative. A number of other practical resources offer possible strategies as well: Arreola (2000, p. 7) discusses ways to construct a "functionally valid" faculty evaluation system, Wergin (2003) gives examples of many types of evidence that can be used to assess pedagogical quality, Seldin (1999) evaluates mechanisms such as teaching portfolios, peer observations, and student feedback, and Ory and Ryan (2002) offer suggestions about ways to enhance the consequential validity of ratings, or what the evaluations signify to users and how they are utilized in personnel decisions. However, the particular mechanisms used are best left up to discussion among a department's faculty and chairs.

CHAPTER FOUR

SOCIAL NETWORKS AS BUILDING BLOCKS FOR CONGRUENCE: FACULTY THAT CHALK TOGETHER TALK TOGETHER

The following piece from the *Chronicle of Higher Education* touts the benefits of research collaborations:

> So what could you possibly gain from collaborating with others as you pursue your scientific goals, exposing yourself to interpersonal conflict like a lab rat to a pathogen? . . . Whether we like it or not, collaboration is becoming the norm for much federally financed research. Sometimes the complexity of today's scientific questions requires investigators from a variety of disciplines to work together. (Markin, 2005)

Indeed, research has indicated that faculty do engage in a number of collaborations around scholarship and that these ties are beneficial. Starting in 1973, Peter Blau argued that academic departments can be locations of tight social networks built around similar research interests. Examining this thesis further, Freidkin (1978) reported instead that a significant proportion of researchers' scholarly connections are interdepartmental, and Etzkowitz, Kemelgor, and Uzzi (2000) found that a high number of interdisciplinary ties has a more positive influence on scientists' research productivity than a similar number of intradepartmental connections. However, there has been no parallel research on faculty's instructional ties.[13]

This chapter examines the teaching networks created by faculty in congruent and incongruent departments. It then examines how organizational structures and practices, such as instructional arrangements and locations in which teaching is discussed, shape these pedagogical webs. Finally, it looks at the composition of these teaching networks, to better understand how gender, race, and nationality also may play a role in their shape. Although congruence is a valuable organizational asset, representing general alignment trends across a department, particular attention also needs to be devoted to specificities, or whether certain individuals are more likely to be left out of teaching networks.

INTERACTION AND DEVELOPMENT
OF SHARED BELIEFS ABOUT TEACHING

Through interaction, faculty are more likely to develop interpretive structures, by coming to agreement about how to operationalize formal teaching standards into shared guidelines for practice. The more faculty talk about teaching, the more opportunities they will have to develop these structures.

Interaction can take two forms: indirect and direct. At one level, simple knowledge of another's beliefs and activities—such as cognizance of another's ideas about teaching—establishes the precondition of visibility necessary for social influence. Even if faculty do not have face-to-face contact, their expressed recognition that colleagues have interesting views about teaching is one important indicator that instructional beliefs are being disseminated.

However, direct contact does have a stronger effect on congruence than indirect identification of an instructional reference. According to those who study social networks, or the patterns of connections within a social group, faculty who have direct contact with peers are more likely to gain understanding of others' beliefs and behaviors and, therefore, come to agreement with them (Erickson, 1988; Gartrell, 1987; Marsden & Friedkin, 1994; Poole & McPhee, 1983; Singer, 1980). Indeed, departments with faculty members who generally talk frequently are also more likely to discuss issues pertaining to undergraduate education specifically (Massy, Wilger, & Colbeck, 1994). Thus, interaction around instructional matters, whether through conversations about teaching or jointly performed activities, is likely to shape congruent beliefs in a department. To give a practical example, Quinlan's (1996, p. 180) research on the impact of teaching circles on academics' beliefs about teaching concludes that "faculty in both departments seemed to gain a better understanding and appreciation of the perspectives of colleagues with whom they normally did not interact." Thus, widespread interaction around instructional matters, whether through conversations about teaching or jointly performed activities, is likely to shape congruent beliefs in a department.

MEASURING TEACHING NETWORKS

For all of the junior faculty I interviewed, I asked two questions: "When you want to talk to someone about teaching, with whom do you speak?" and, at the conclusion of the interview, "Are there other people I should speak with who would have an interesting or valuable perspective on these issues?" In addition to noting direct responses to these questions, I also noted in the remainder of the interview when respondents mentioned other instructional encounters with faculty.[14]

To explore the shape and impact of junior faculty's teaching ties, I constructed instructional networks linking faculty references. Many social network methodologists advise the use of highly systematized surveys or interviews to solicit names, a multidirectional analysis of interactions between all members of the social group in question, and a heavily quantitative analysis of the data to explore characteristics such as centrality and density (e.g., Burt, 1980; Scott, 2000). The more qualitative approach used here diverges from this system for three important reasons. First, solicitation of names took place in the context of a forty-minute semi-structured interview. Because of varying beliefs about what constitutes teaching in a research university (Blackburn et al., 1980; Boice, 1991, 1992; Fink, 1984; Goodwin & Stevens, 1993; Mann, 1970), it was necessary to contextualize faculty's responses to better understand when a respondent perceived that instructional interactions or conversations had occurred. Second, junior faculty's instructional references were analyzed unidirectionally; in other words, only references named by assistant professors were included in the network. It was necessary to limit the analysis to one rank to avoid the impact of demographic composition on faculty consensus (Lawrence, 1984). Finally, because there was a relatively small pool of respondents, a complex quantitative analysis was unnecessary. In fact, the resulting numbers become richer when interpreted through a qualitative lens, supplemented by other findings from the interviews.

With the resulting names, an instructional network of the faculty mentioned was constructed. Behavioral links (to whom respondents talk about or observe teaching) were differentiated from cognitive reference groups (who has an interesting view about teaching), on the grounds that the direct contact indicated by the former would be more likely to produce agreement (Erickson, 1988; Gartrell, 1987; Marsden & Friedkin, 1994; Poole & McPhee, 1983; Singer, 1980). Only four individuals were referenced external to the four departments, three by faculty who had a joint appointment in another unit. Unlike the interdisciplinary connections needed for research activity, it appears that faculty seek out teaching connections that are more particular to their home departments. This finding is consistent with research showing that teaching involves a local orientation (Blau, 1973; Gouldner, 1957).

Differences in Networks

The instructional networks named by junior faculty in the congruent and incongruent departments show some differences. Professors in congruent

Table 6. Teaching Ties

	Congruent Departments		Incongruent Departments	
	Number	Mean per Asst. Prof.	Number	Mean per Asst. Prof.
Total Number of Ties	67	7.4	43	5.4
Number of Faculty Identified	35	3.9	26	3.3
Behavioral Ties	25	2.8	14	1.8

departments identified one and one-half times more instructional links than did faculty in incongruent units, sixty-seven versus forty-three, an average of two additional names per respondent (Table 6). However, mean differences in the number of separate faculty names are slight: 3.9 and 3.3 for the congruent and incongruent units, respectively. Congruent units also showed a slight advantage in the number of behavioral ties, which are more likely to elicit understanding of and agreement about instructional beliefs.

Overall, congruent departments show slightly more extensive instructional networks. However, these general patterns mask some important differences. An important qualification lies in the number of people named, in spite of the relatively equal size of the departments in terms of instructional staff. Faculty whom multiple respondents referenced as sources of teaching information are here termed *instructional leaders*. Although the total number of faculty identified is only slightly larger in the congruent departments, their networks contain many more instructional leaders. Separate congruent department faculty repeated five faculty names twice and identified four names three times. In contrast, incongruent units repeated two faculty names twice, but one professor received mentions from four respondents (Table 7). Therefore, congruent departments had more instructional leaders, while incongruent units had fewer and, in one case, more frequently referenced people.

Table 7. Instructional Leaders

No. Faculty Referenced:	Congruent Departments	Incongruent Departments
Two Times	5	2
Three Times	4	0
Four Times	0	1

WHAT ARE REASONS FOR DIFFERENCES
IN TEACHING NETWORKS?

The instructional networks named by junior faculty in the congruent departments show some small advantages in size and extensiveness. These findings are consistent with research conducted by social network theorists, which finds that those who have direct contact with colleagues are more likely to agree with their beliefs (Erickson, 1988; Gartrell, 1987; Marsden & Friedkin, 1994; Poole & McPhee, 1983; Singer, 1980). The greater degree to which the teaching network permeated through congruent units would allow for more cross-departmental interaction around instructional issues, thereby affording faculty more opportunities to come to agreement about the value of teaching and the ways in which effective teaching should be defined as a unit.

However, a more significant difference may be the varying number of instructional leaders. Faculty in incongruent units named fewer faculty as instructional references, and one professor was very frequently identified. The centralization of a network is an indication of the degree to which information is concentrated (Trotter, 1999). Therefore, the lower number of frequently identified instructional references in incongruent units would allow for a less dispersed spread of information about teaching standards.

Patterns of interaction can be profoundly shaped by organizational structures. For example, office location, inclusiveness of administrative meetings, and teaching arrangements either can promote fluid interaction among faculty across a department or limit such comparisons to subgroups or cliques. As indicated by educational researchers, organizational structures that can facilitate interaction are practices such as collective review of student ratings, peer review of teaching, team teaching, and regular programs on pedagogical topics (Bess, 2000; Cuban, 1999; Feldman & Paulsen, 1999; Matney, 2001; Quinlan, 1996; Quinn, 1994; Rice & Austin, 1990; Woods, 1999). I turn to qualitative data to understand how instructional information came to be located in the hands of a few in incongruent departments, and how congruent departments construct more extensive networks.

Reasons for Concentration of Instructional Information

As described in chapter 1's history of the Star Department, this unit recently had undertaken an extensive curriculum reform project for its undergraduate and graduate programs. Much of work for this reform was spearheaded by three faculty members: two have since retired while another continues to work for the university. The latter faculty member has assumed near-mythical status in the department: Every respondent mentioned this person's name during the course of the interview or recommended this person as someone with whom I should speak. The stories told about this person noted her/his unique tenure case and valuable work in the department:

> This [discipline] department is unusual because we have a full-time
> faculty member tenured whose focus is education [in the disci-
> pline]. . . . Everybody who has ever worked with her/him when he/
> she is [a course] coordinator worships her/him. He/she is so good.

It would be overstating the case to say that all activity around instructional
issues is directed by one person; for example, one respondent was involved
in an undergraduate course reform, and some others did significant work with
graduate students. However, all of these people mentioned that they often
consulted this faculty member or worked under the auspices of a program
that the instructor organized.

In the other incongruent unit, the Divided Department, two instructional actors emerged as having a significant role. The first was the chair.
Part of this department head's prominence stems from the organizational
structure of the department: the associate chair position in this unit had
been eliminated (by the chair), and the only other governing faculty was a
seven-person elected committee that had no voting power but played an
advisory role. However, the chair's importance stems from more than formal
bureaucratic position. Faculty describe this administrator's relationship with
them in many different contexts, mentioning "good rapport," guidance in
tenure matters, encouragement, and flexibility. Many faculty depicted the
chair's role in tenure and promotion procedures as significant, not only in
making the final decision but also in guiding the applicant through the
process. One respondent told a story that is illustrative of the influence the
chair has throughout these administrative processes:

> When I interviewed for this job, [the chair] said, "I am going to take
> your success as a personal matter." [The chair] meant that. Not all
> chairs do that. A lot of people just throw you out there to the lions,
> and it is a sink or swim situation. [The chair] took it as a personal goal
> to help me. Because of those rare supportive people [like the chair],
> I was able to know [what I needed to succeed in the department].

Because there were few in the department who were near to the tenure
process, initial conversations with the chair were the most valuable way
assistant professors learned about departmental expectations. Even tenured
faculty echoed the central role of this administrator, especially in summative
evaluations of teaching.

While the chair plays a central role in communicating, monitoring,
and enforcing instructional standards for the department, another key actor
was identified primarily for practice. In this unit, faculty perceived an opportunity cost to large didactic courses, and time devoted to managing the
course was time that could have been spent on research. As a result, only

one faculty member, a senior member of the department, took responsibility for much of the didactic teaching.

Attributable primarily to organizational arrangements or historical patterns in instructional work, both of these incongruent departments employed one or two people who held extraordinarily prominent teaching roles. A system of disseminating information, like a radio broadcast, relies upon the spread of information from one focal faculty member or administrator to other members of the department, through personal influence and contact. This high degree of centralization may come at the cost of faculty interpersonal interaction. Because instructional standards and responsibilities are so clearly located in one or two points, colleagues may have less of a need or opportunity to look to each other to construct their own understandings of effective teaching. As an ironic illustration of this dynamic, when I asked one Star Department professor about what the unit does to encourage faculty to spend time and effort on their instructional roles, this respondent told me that he was too busy to know—but "the star" would know the answer to my question!

Reasons for Extensiveness of Instructional Information

While incongruent departments tended to have few leaders who concentrated instructional information, congruent units demonstrated a more diffuse teaching network. This dispersed information flow indicates that the units allow for more opportunities to interact around teaching-related issues, affording more chances for faculty to come to agreement about instructional matters. The following section discusses what congruent departments do differently to foster more extensive instructional interactions.

Team Teaching

In examining the instructional arrangements that are associated with congruence, team teaching emerged as an extraordinarily significant theme. Through team teaching, faculty could directly observe and communicate with colleagues in order to make judgments as to what constitutes effective teaching. To put it as a bumper sticker might, faculty that chalk together talk together.

Both congruent departments utilized extensive team teaching arrangements, although they took quite different forms. In the Universe Department, faculty manned discussion sections of the large courses that served as the anchor for the unit's undergraduate enrollment. Although this was not team teaching in its formal sense—that is, multiple faculty leading a course simultaneously—course directors and section leaders did interact outside of the classroom to plan and coordinate the course. This modified team teaching structure played both a symbolic and functional role for faculty. While faculty felt that professor-run discussion sections symbolized the value the department accorded to undergraduate teaching, the arrangement also allowed for communication around instructional issues. For example, one respondent reported, "People that will be doing discussions or teaching their courses often talk to one another. And it's a common topic of conversation. It can be a common topic of conversation about how it's going for you and how it's going for me or discussions the instructor might have with how their discussion section goes when it's unique to them."

Faculty in the Team Unit utilized a more traditional team teaching approach, often instructing courses in groups of two or more. Rather than have an instructor teach a course on her specialty, the department chose to stretch its personnel resources so that several faculty would lead parts of a course. Additionally, because of the heavily clinical nature of teaching in the department, many courses necessarily required multiple instructors to supervise students.

In contrast, relatively few faculty in the incongruent departments highlighted team teaching as an integral part of their instructional practices. Some faculty did report team teaching practices, but in a qualified manner, describing them as "tag team" teaching. In other words, there was little interaction between instructors; instead, each person gave a lecture at the appointed time in the syllabus.

Peer Review

Peer review, both summative and formative, was another practice that was more highly emphasized in congruent departments than in incongruent units. In the Universe Department, peer review took place through a multitiered system, by which assistant professors could learn about instructional expectations from multiple members. In this system, personnel committee members visited the classrooms of assistant professors once per term. Mentors, senior faculty in the department who were assigned to assistant professors upon hire, also are required to evaluate the course. Other faculty-administrators, such as associate chairs and chairs, could add a third perspective if needed.

In the Team Department, peer review practices might be described as formative, or perhaps more aptly, *performative*, or taken-for-granted departmental practices of classroom visitations. Because teaching was heavily structured around sequential courses, overlapping instructors, and team teaching, it was possible for all faculty to be effective observers nearly all of the time; they could gather information about what others were doing in the classroom. This instructional organization enabled all faculty to, as one respondent related, "see each other teaching or at least see what the students know by sitting in other people's classes." As another faculty member explained, this system afforded faculty an opportunity to gather data on their colleagues' instructional views and practices:

> I have sat in on not everybody's classes. There are a couple that I have not sat in on. But I have sat in on almost everybody's. Not to be nosy but because I wanted to see the content of the course and how the course flowed.

As a result of the department's generalist orientation and interactive instructional practices, there is a high degree of communication among faculty about instructional matters.

In contrast, in the incongruent departments, peer review was not implemented or was deemphasized by faculty. In the Star Department, three members indicated in interviews that peer review was required of assistant and associate professors in the department. However, one never experienced the process:

> I was told that as an assistant professor, observers from the department and the [college] committees would regularly walk into courses I would be teaching. I was told this but it never happened. . . . So I am not sure how that assessment actually happens.

Another, who taught a laboratory class, said that the observation was not required of such a course. The only participant who had gone through such a review found that "it's not very useful feedback" because there was a lag of several months between when the peer evaluation was done and when he received a report on the process. To further emphasize the disconnect, in contrast to the faculty perspective, the chair was surprised to hear about experiences with peer review, because he thought the practice had been discontinued in the department.

In the Divided Department, faculty indicated that there were some unique structural barriers in the department that made it difficult for them to assess colleagues' subject matter knowledge. Many faculty—even the chair—did not have doctorates in the field taught by the department; instead, the department was a veritable melting pot of scientific disciplines. Such disciplinary variety made peer review more difficult, as a professor explained: "There are a lot of people who are true experts on the things that they know, and some of them have almost no peer or a small number of people to whom they might compare themselves." In fact, many respondents did feel that peer review was a less-than-perfect system, as one related:

> Typically, what often happens is that people audit classes, I know some of our faculty audit each other's classes, and see how effective they are, and I know that the chair takes particular interest in how well the courses are being run, and I know that [the chair's] gone to some lectures and sat in on them. But it's very difficult. It's not like taking an exam.

In contrast to review by their peers, some respondents did feel that evaluations conducted by the chair were useful, which, again, is indicative of the central role this administrative head plays in setting such standards.

Locations of Instructional Discussions

Across departments, faculty identified three venues in which discussions about instructional matters took place: formal colloquia or brownbags, administrative meetings, and informal conversations or gatherings. Some congruent faculty reported infrequent colloquia and administrative discussion of instructional matters, but these were not highlighted as significant arenas for discussion. One Universe professor explained, "Every now and again we have a colloquium from someone who is involved in teaching matters, but that would be once a year maybe and it's not quite thought to be the thing to do." Although some faculty with more administrative roles perceived committee discussions to be valuable, for most professors, it was the everyday, unstructured conversations that were most useful:

> We do also have a departmental committee, which looks at issues in the undergraduate program, and another committee that looks at issues in the graduate courses. And some of these things are discussed there. But for the most part, as with most committees, that's not really where things happen. It's really the people talking to themselves and doing something, you know, coming up with some ideas on their own.

Faculty indicated that instructional conversations took place in such venues as a department's daily afternoon coffee break or in the hallways.

In a research-oriented department, how did faculty broach the subject of teaching with colleagues? Respondents indicated that the most common initiator of these conversations was a general inquiry about "How is it going?" It was felt that this type of teaching question could be, and was, asked of almost any faculty member in the department. Additionally, content-related instructional questions could be directed to any colleague. Only if specific questions about pedagogical techniques arose did respondents delimit the group of people with whom they were likely to speak. For example, one member specified, "Well, you have informal conversations with all colleagues on the faculty of just how it's going this term. You know, 'What are you doing?' But if I want to have a more formal discussion about, 'Should I teach this course next year?' 'Would it be a good idea to do that?' 'Should I try this or that approach to lecturing?' 'Should I give this or that type of exam?,' I would ask [names of five colleagues]."

In contrast, in the incongruent departments, delimited conversations always took on greater importance. Administrative spaces, such as subspecialty meetings, were reported as the most frequent location where discussions about teaching occurred. With such a large group of faculty, the department relies heavily upon a decision-making process that farms out decisions through smaller gatherings of faculty, or seven groups that are divided by academic subspecialty. Some of these groups were reported to discuss teaching and some were not. However, because these formal meetings were more likely to take place among a subset of faculty, such as faculty in one research specialty, there was less opportunity for cross-departmental influence. Clearly, informal interactions could be constricted in a similar manner, shaped by factors such as office location or personal proclivities. However, there was not the same level of restriction of association as, for example, an executive committee meeting.

The preceding section emphasized the importance of routines and structures—such as team teaching, frequent interactions, and informal sharing—on instructional congruence. Interestingly, many of these practices are identified in work that examines constituents of productive and inclusive *research* environments. As Bilmoria and Jordan (2005, p. 2) note, "Scientists achieve good science through interactions that provide and generate resources." (See also Bland, Weber-Main, Lund, & Finstad, 2005.) There can be an elision between research and teaching in the sciences, especially at the graduate level (Wright, 2002). As one of my respondents noted, "We do our research, but we do it in a teaching format," so for example, a lab experience would also be a mentorship of graduate students and some undergraduate assistants. Therefore, it makes sense that benefits accrued in instructional congruence would transfer to scholarship, and vice versa.

WHO IS LEFT OUT?

In the four departments studied here, there were clear patterns of congruence and incongruence. However, even within the highly congruent "teams," where most members feel their own beliefs align with those of the department, there exist some instructors who watch from the sidelines, feeling marginal to these organizations. These isolates do not participate in the interactive networks that other faculty do. They do not feel they understand promotion policies as well as other faculty, nor do they feel as valued for their instruction. In turn, they do not believe that the unit values teaching. At first only physically isolated, they become increasingly perceived as "loners," more culturally isolated and less valued. Who is more likely to be isolated, and how do they get that way? The following sections take a more in-depth look at overall network patterns to examine the role that gender, race, and nationality play in shaping them.

Gender

Women and minorities often are excluded from professional networks, which has consequences not only for their own career advancement but also for a department's capacities to facilitate direct social engagement around instructional matters (Boice, 1993a, 1993b; Johnsrud & Wunsc, 1991; Sonnert, 1995; Tierney & Bensimon, 1996). In the sciences, this exclusion may have additional ramifications, because of expectations that faculty are expected to interact to communicate findings, evaluate peers, and garner resources (Traweek, 1988). Indeed, research on scientific networks shows that women are not, or do not feel they are, included in collegial research networks necessary to advance in their fields (Davis, 2001; Etzkowitz, Kemelgor, & Uzzi, 2000; Rose, 1989).

However, given that women are expected to value and spend more time on teaching than men, might the dynamics be reversed in the case of instructional networks (Finkelstein, 1984; Finkelstein, Seal, & Schuster, 1998; Sax, Astin, Korn, & Gilmartin,1999)? Significantly more often than men, women report that they consult with colleagues to help improve their teaching (Goodwin & Stevens, 1993). It may be that while women are excluded more often from research connections, they are more integral to a department's instructional network.

Table 8 indicates that among the four departments, there is some variability by gender composition. Interestingly, this pattern does not seem to map onto congruence, with congruent departments containing both the highest and the lowest proportion of female faculty.

However, to get a better sense of how gender influenced respondents' instructional networks, the number of female or male faculty named as instructional references was divided by the total number of male or female fulltime tenure-track or clinical faculty in the department. (This denominator is henceforth referred to as "possible" male or female faculty.)

Overall, a slightly greater proportion (47 percent) of possible female faculty than male faculty (40 percent) in the four departments were named as instructional referents, although this percentage varied widely by unit. Faculty in the most congruent department in this study, the Team Department, named 100 percent of possible women as part of their instructional networks, and it also was the only department to have well over a critical mass of female faculty, a level usually placed at 15 percent (Etzkowitz,

Table 8. Gender Composition of Departments

	Percent Gender Composition of Department (excluding Emeriti)	
	% Male	% Female
Universe Department	95%	5%
Divided Department	85%	15%
Star Department	89%	11%
Team Department	70%	30%

Kemelgor, & Uzzi, 2000; Kanter, 1977). In turn, faculty in the most incongruent unit, the Divided Department, named the lowest proportion of possible female faculty, 25 percent. (About 15 percent of the Divided Department's faculty were female.)

In sum, these findings suggest that departments that effectively maintain a culture of congruence *and* recruit and retain female faculty also contain instructional networks that are gender inclusive. After all, congruence involves a sense that one can identify with one's colleagues or organization, and a group with only a token representation of women is more likely to construct a culture that emphasizes gender differences (Kanter, 1977). Even though women might be expected to value and spend more time on teaching than men, in such skewed settings, it is less likely that women will be included in men's social and professional gatherings. Therefore, without a significant representation of women in the academic unit, female faculty will tend not to be named as reference points.

Academic units with a critical mass (greater than 15 percent of female faculty) and a "relational" culture have a positive impact on women's development of research networks (Etzkowitz, Kemelgor, & Uzzi, 2000). Interestingly, similar factors, representation and culture, seem to have a positive influence on women's instructional networks as well. This may result because collectivistic organizational cultures tend to encourage interaction around demographically dissimilar people (Chatman, Polzer, Barsade, & Neale, 1998).

Nationality

Even within congruent departments, three of those I interviewed identified themselves as being marginal to their units in some regard: they had recently been denied tenure or they felt that their professional responsibilities differed from those of their colleagues. Interestingly, two of these three respondents were not perceived as marginal by their junior or senior colleagues, at least in terms of instructional issues—they often were named as someone people talked to about teaching or even someone who was "valued."

All of these isolates were of a different nationality than the majority of the department, they worked in distant offices, and, consequently, they networked with fewer colleagues. In turn, their responses more closely resembled those of faculty who were employed in incongruent departments in that they felt that their beliefs about teaching were not shared with colleagues.

As any real estate agent could tell you, location is key. Isolates tended to work in locations that were physically distant from their colleagues. All of the offices were situated in out-of-the-way hallways or in a different building altogether from the one in which the rest of the department gathered. Often, I was nearly late to interviews held in these three faculty's offices, because they were in such hard-to-find places! One isolate noted, "I spend a lot of time isolated in the [site miles from the department], because I'm the only person there." Likewise, another marginalized faculty member, who is more involved in research than other members of the department, has a laboratory in an office that is located far away from the main facility. As a result, this faculty member faces the same problem of lack of opportunities for interaction: "The problem is that I don't see anything. Our department . . . I hardly see anyone. I am up here on my own. I don't see anybody around."

Second, all of these faculty are foreign nationals. This status was perceived to have an impact on collegial interactions, as one respondent reported: "People, of course, want to say, no, we treat everybody equally. But, it's there, and it's very easy to feel if you are a foreign national, if you will. And I think it's only something that those who are foreign national, those who have been on that kind of situation can tell." To be fair, other respondents who were foreign nationals did not report the same attitudes. However, it may be that taken together with other isolating forces, having a different nationality becomes a more salient differentiating factor. In combination, these influences work to set apart faculty so that they feel isolated from the main group.

The resulting isolation impacts these faculty members' beliefs about teaching: while most professors report that instruction is highly valued in the unit, the stance of these respondents differs significantly. To illustrate, one described how the unit professed a value for effective teaching, yet paid only token support to the activity: "I want to become a better teacher, I know I have a lot, lot of room to improve. And I'm not given that opportunity here. The [college] says that teaching is very valuable. But they really need to make that clear to us and provide ways in which we can really grow and do the stuff that we can do. . . . If you don't really make room for those of us who are carrying the school, in terms of the teaching, to grow and really become effective teachers, then it's just lip service." While this instructor described a deviation from one aspect of congruence, the rating of the department and colleagues, the second marginal member indicated a misalignment in the second respect, self-evaluation of instruction. "I am not happy in this environment," this respondent felt. Continuing, she noted that "in terms of effective teaching here, I am struggling how to teach better." This respondent indicated a frustration with teaching, to a point where "I am not even going to bother to try. I say forget it." The third did not get tenure.

Left out of the departments' strong teaching networks, the marginal faculty questioned both their own teaching ability and the commitment of their department to teaching. Differentiated by their unique physical locations, work responsibilities, and nationalities, these faculty are not fully incorporated into the instructional relationships that take place between the chair and most other faculty. Indeed, when looking at their instructional networks, these faculty understood their own web of connections to contain relatively few members as compared to their peers. Additionally, they had no behavioral ties, the stronger teaching connection. As a result of this lack of integration, isolates' understandings of the unit's or their own value for teaching differed significantly from their colleagues who are tied more strongly to the department.

Race and Ethnicity

Measuring the faculty participation of racial and ethnic minorities in networks is difficult, as the number of faculty belonging to underrepresented groups is very small and information about faculty's racial/ethnic identity is limited. I can offer only the observation that even in departments with minority senior faculty, many were not mentioned as part of the department's teaching networks. This may mean that like foreign nationals, members of racial and ethnic minorities can find themselves isolated in departments. It also might indicate that in an effort to counteract other barriers to success, minority faculty feel they need to focus less on teaching in order to survive in a research-oriented environment (Tierney & Bensimon, 1996).

CONCLUSION: CONGRUENCE AS INSTRUMENT MAKING

In the following narrative, an organizational researcher describes the workings of a company that makes musical instruments:

> Imagine that you are watching people seated side by side, working at a table, making flutes. One person is holding the long tube into which tone holes have been drilled, forming the body of the flute. She is affixing to it the structure that holds the key mechanism. When she finishes her work, she passes it to the next flutemaker. . . . At every point along this "line," as a piece is passed, each maker assesses the work of the previous flutemaker. If the flute "does not feel right," . . . the worker will say so while handing the piece back to the previous flutemaker for further work. (Yanow, 2000, p. 249; see also Cook & Yanow, 1993)

Each worker, through interaction and communication, learns the collective criteria of an "effective" instrument. Apprentices develop into expert craftspeople through the group process of the passing back of each flute component. How are congruent departments like these manufacturers?

Perhaps it is best to start with how faculty are not like them. Most instructional work occurs in isolation, with each faculty member teaching his or her own course. In many cases, there are not opportunities for developing a learning organization like the Powell Flute Company—imagine faculty teaching in one room, returning a student to the instructor of a previous course, remarking that the learning "doesn't feel right"! Then why, if faced with similar ambiguity about teaching in the research university context, do faculty ever agree about teaching?

The difference for congruent departments may lie in occasions for faculty and administrators to become like the instrument makers: opportunities to interact around instructional issues. Like this workplace, congruent departments have constructed communities in which faculty can discuss teaching and determine the criteria for an "effective" performance. In this study, congruent units differed from incongruent departments in the greater size, extensiveness, and number of instructional leaders in their networks. The network structure in congruent departments suggests that faculty have greater cross-departmental interaction around instructional issues, affording more opportunities for alignment. The highly concentrated instructional work in incongruent departments, located in the hands of one or two people and discussed primarily in administrative venues, may set the stage for a network structure that limits faculty interaction. In contrast, interviews with faculty in congruent units indicate that their network structures may be associated with the following departmental practices: team teaching, peer review, and frequent and informal instructional discussions.

These constituents of congruence also are identified by others as structures that support teaching cultures (Bess, 2000; Cuban, 1999; Feldman & Paulsen, 1999; Paulsen & Feldman, 1995; Quinlan, 1996; Quinn, 1994). However, it is important to note that this study emphasizes that informal practices and interactions take on as much salience in shaping faculty's perceptions of their departmental culture as do formal policies and procedures. For example, performative practices had effects similar to a formal peer review system. While congruent departments did not sponsor regular forums on pedagogical topics, everyday conversations about teaching played a significant role in shaping faculty's beliefs about teaching.

What are the implications for administrators and faculty who wish to cultivate a culture of instructional congruence? First, these findings suggest that successful measures often are ones that do not add significantly to faculty and administrators' workloads. For example, informal conversations about instructional issues are extremely important for fostering congruence. Second, chairs and meso-level administrators have a role in facilitating widespread activity when a department decides to engage in curricular work. Designation of a teaching "expert," who often is called upon to spearhead the administrative and experiential instructional work of a department, can concentrate instructional information in an incongruent manner. Third, faculty and administrators can support authentic intradepartmental team teaching. Fourth, faculty and chairs can develop and recommend peer review opportunities, whether they are summative, formative, or performative. Finally, by being attentive to differentiating factors, whether structural (e.g., office location) or social (e.g., diversity), chairs can attenuate the isolating factors that distance some faculty, even in a congruent department.

CHAPTER FIVE

HOW CHAIRS BUILD INSTRUCTIONAL

COMMUNITIES: BIG PICTURES

VERSUS BIG IMPACTS

A recent piece from the *Chronicle of Higher Education* narrates a story told from the perspective of a new academic chair:

> I spend most of my time dealing with the urgent or the mundane and sometimes the "urgent mundane"—resolving a teacher-student issue, finding storage space for files and equipment, answering e-mails from administrators, lining up adjunct instructors, listening to a colleague's complaints, advising and registering students. . . . The important "big picture" issues that I envisioned myself doing as a department head—like planning for the future, budgeting, managing finances, corresponding, and writing portions of the self-study for the accreditation review—are pushed to the bottom of the pile. I deal with such "important" items in the fragments of time I have between appointments and other responsibilities. (Franklin, 2005)

In many departments, the role of teaching often ends up as a "big picture" issue that never gets addressed—or, to continue the metaphor, relegated only to the "coming attractions." Ann Lucas's (1989) research indicates that improving the quality of teaching in the department and developing faculty commitment to departmental goals are the top responses to the question she poses in her workshops: "What would it take to make yours a high quality department?" However, only a minority of chairs report that they are successful at these aims.

In spite of these challenges, the chair literature continues to recommend that chairs continue to place teaching on the big picture agenda. Lucas

(1989) herself suggests that department chairs schedule a workshop on teaching, in order to develop faculty commitment to instruction. Others advise that chairs shift meeting agenda away from "administrivia" to a broader discussion about the department's values in regard to research, teaching, and service (Hecht, Higgerson, Gmelch, & Tucker, 1999). However, how are chairs to move to these big picture questions, if the role itself is so pressure-filled that it has been described as "a block of wood in a vice" (Seagren, Wheeler, & Creswell, 1993, p. iii)?

Indeed, my work on teaching cultures in research universities suggests that leaving instructional discussions to the highly ceremonial, big picture events—such as the "faculty meeting when our values about teaching will be discussed" or the "pedagogical colloquium when we finally will have a chance to talk about teaching"—has a deleterious effect on this endeavor. Often, the message the chair wishes to convey can be interpreted differently by faculty, or most of the department may not even attend. Instead, I argue that most of the time, department chairs can best cultivate a culture of teaching through small, informal efforts that clarify the department's instructional standards and values. These small activities help to set the stage so that if a chair does want to engage the department in a formal, big picture event, it will be valued by faculty.

An effective and supportive chair can be an important constituent of a teaching culture (Feldman & Paulsen, 1999; Cuban, 1999; Rice & Austin, 1990; Lucas, 1990). However, it is also true that chairs often perceive themselves as being more supportive to faculty than do the faculty themselves (Whitt, 1991). Clearly, faculty can play significant roles in developing these organizational structures in departments, and I will return to those roles at the end of this book. However, because many of these arrangements often are highly shaped by chairs, this chapter is devoted to the part administrative heads play in constructing a culture of congruence. How can chairs effectively cultivate a culture of instructional congruence?

Earlier, I noted how faculty in congruent departments created more extensive teaching networks, which, I argue, helps to facilitate shared beliefs about teaching. Chapter 4 focuses on three departmental activities that were conducive to the creation of instructional ties: team teaching, peer review of teaching, and talking about teaching in everyday conversations. Additionally, chapter 3 notes that chairs play a key role in helping faculty to interpret policies and means of evaluating teaching. Chairs clearly play a significant role in structuring all of these activities into department policy and practice. However, in this section, I will elaborate on the moments in which departments talk about teaching, because chairs figure into this activity so extensively and because instructional discussions are so critical to organizational congruence. I also will identify how chairs' conceptualizations of their roles figure into developing a culture of instructional congruence.

In this study, the self-described and perceived role of the chair varied widely by type of department. In the smaller professional and graduate-oriented units (in the health sciences), the chair role was very strong and central. In contrast, the large undergraduate units described a leadership structure with several layers, as well as a decision-making system largely driven by consensus. Congruence emerged in both the centralized decision-making structures and in the consensus-based systems, but the key difference was how effectively chairs were able to cultivate extensive instructional contacts and mobilize highly symbolic events to communicate the value of teaching.

Differences in graduate departments: Centralized leadership

The health science departments' leadership structures were similar in their centralized power. Both chairs worked with advisory teams, who had no voting powers. Although these units had section heads or directors, they did not have an assistant/associate chair structure to delegate responsibilities. For example, one head described the role in a "buck stops here" manner: "In the final analysis, I want to make the decisions, because I was given the authority by the dean, and if there is a mistake made, I will be the one who is responsible." Similarly, the other chair's style was frequently described as "where [the department] is a wheel, and he is in the center, as opposed to being committee-related."

In addition to this centralized authority, both leaders also felt it important to develop what Sally Helgeson (1995, p. 6) terms "interactive charisma," or "a way of leading that derives power and authority from being accessible." To illustrate, faculty in both departments noted the chairs' open door policies.

However, there was a key difference in how the "open door policy" was enacted, resulting in a much greater interactive style for the congruent department chair. In other words, the locations of instructional discussions—formal colloquia or brownbags, administrative meetings, and informal conversations or gatherings—are as much a preference of faculty in the department as a deliberate strategy of the chair. In the incongruent Divided Department, the chair was accessible, but faculty needed to come to him: "Everybody knows that I have an open door policy. That doesn't mean they use it." In contrast, a division head in the congruent department noted that hallway conversations—in other words, "excursions" by the chair out of the office—were most utilized in the department. He noted that the advantage is that you "don't wait for a discussion that is unpredictable, that may never happen."

A second key difference was how teaching was framed by the chairs at public events. In the congruent Team Department, teaching was rarely discussed at formal administrative meetings. However, because the chair's open door policy was seen as being so effective, this lack of discussion was not perceived as problematic. For example, a faculty member in this unit noted, "So, there's no formal department thing about teaching but there doesn't need to be because the people are so accessible. I just literally walk into [the chair's] office."

In contrast, in the incongruent unit, teaching was more frequently discussed at formal gatherings such as retreats, faculty meetings, and committee meetings. However, most of these discussions were framed in terms of logistical and curricular matters—developing a new program or discussing who should teach what—and as result, faculty did not feel that "big teaching issues" were addressed by the unit, even though the chair thought they were. For example, the chair remarked, "There's a lot of discussion about graduate teaching." However, an experienced faculty member noted, "As an organizational unit, we spend very little time talking about the value of teaching." Additionally, a newer member of the department also echoed this sentiment: "I don't think that people talk a great deal about it." Therefore, even though teaching was on the agendas of these events, they were not framed symbolically to emphasize to faculty that discussions addressed the value of teaching in the department.

Differences in undergraduate departments: Leadership by consensus

Both undergraduate science departments' leadership structures were quite different from the graduate departments'. These departments were larger, and their college's culture was characterized by more decentralized leadership. Therefore, the chair's decision-making capabilities were delegated to assistant or associate chairs and limited by executive committees with voting powers. These chairs conceptualized their role more as coordinators: one who can "suggest" or "collect" agenda items and interact democratically with the faculty to move issues forward.

Also different from the graduate units, both chairs saw symbolic implications in their roles, noting that they needed to communicate that good teaching was valued. However, this process of communication was much more concrete in the congruent department.

The incongruent Star Department chair described his role as instilling a "sense of value and importance to good teaching." When asked how he did this, the chair mentioned face-to-face meetings with individuals and some messages conveyed to key committees. However, this administrative head felt that his approach had limited effectiveness. "You can't make anyone do anything," he noted, you can "only suggest." One way that good teaching was "suggested" was through the department's series on teaching, modeled after a research-type seminar. However, during my observations of these seminars, very few faculty were in attendance. Rooted primarily in administrative formalities, the chair's symbolic message had its limitations.

In contrast, the congruent Universe Department chair described very specific political strategies designed to get faculty's buy-in regarding teaching. For example, the chair taught every year—something not to be taken for granted in a large research university science department—because continuing to teach was "absolutely vital" to maintain credibility from colleagues. Faculty noted this symbolism, and I heard from several faculty that the chair performed "extremely well" and did a "top gun, bang up job." This success supported his conviction that valuable departmental members were those who "pull their weight," meaning that the teaching load was carefully assessed and reassigned when someone was not doing enough teaching. Beyond these formal measures, the chair also reinforced the messages through informal communication channels. During our interview, he noted that refreshments for the daily afternoon coffee break were an important budget item because the informal meeting time was a profitable way to spread information about research and teaching.

LEADERSHIP AUTHORITY AND DISCUSSIONS ABOUT TEACHING

Bolman and Deal (2003) describe eight ways in which leaders derive power, including bureaucratic authority, charisma, and even coercion. According to advice popularly given to chairs, one of these eight, agenda setting, is the most effective way to cultivate a culture of instruction. However, as seen in the popular press, time required to carry out more "pressing" chair functions can be an extremely effective disincentive to putting teaching squarely on the agenda of meetings and formal events. Additionally, as I argued above, even if teaching does reach the agenda of a program or faculty meeting, faculty may not attend nor interpret events as a chair would wish.

Instead, for chairs located in congruent departments, key strategies were building alliances and networks, complemented by the framing of meaning (Bolman & Deal, 2003). The idea that teaching was a meaningful activity was cultivated through highly visible symbolic acts, such as continuing to teach despite a heavy administrative load, as well as frequent informal contacts.

A cultural approach to departments as organizations examines the way in which departments create "networks of meaning" to interpret their work (Moran & Volkwein, 1992, p. 36). This perspective aligns with the strain of leadership theory that sees leadership as a meaning-making activity. With these highly visible acts or frequent informal contacts, chairs are "generating a point of reference, against which a feeling of organization and direction can emerge" (Smircich & Morgan, 1983, p. 258). This point of reference serves as a valuable anchor in a research university, where the role of teaching is often highly ambiguous.

Therefore, what advice can be offered to busy chairs who wish to cultivate a culture of instructional congruence? Administrative heads need to think carefully about any big picture events: Will faculty attend? What meaning will be conveyed by the event? Perhaps more effectively, chairs should look toward big *impact* activities that can be fit into a tight schedule, such as everyday discussions with faculty. Some literature describes this strategy as "management by walking around," or strolls through hallways to facilitate information exchanges (Lees, 2006; Mallard, 1999).

This book has emphasized the key role that chairs play in communicating formal instructional standards and in assisting faculty to interact around teaching matters. Clearly, such communication must go beyond pointing junior faculty to Web sites or manuals that detail tenure processes. Both accessibility (an open door) and outreach (going beyond the door) are useful for chairs to make valuable contacts with faculty.

This approach closely resembles advice for new faculty about writing (Boice, 1992). Writing projects are most effectively completed if one makes available small increments of time each day, rather than scheduling for a large block of time at unpredictable frequencies. Likewise, it is efficacious for administrators to initiate informal, frequent conversations about instructional issues with faculty, rather than to wait for formal discussions at the rare pedagogical event.

Chairs and faculty-administrators in congruent departments facilitated this interaction by such practices as meeting with faculty both annually (on a formal basis) and frequently throughout the year (on an informal basis), and by inserting instructional issues into everyday informal conversations. As we saw in previous chapters, they also broke formal procedures into an easily recognizable set of buzzwords (e.g., "50 percent:30 percent:20 percent for allocation to research, teaching and service activities), utilized a wide variety of techniques for measuring teaching quality, and distributed instructional work widely across the department.

Second, time-intensive, symbolic activities also played a key role in constructing a culture of congruence, but only if they were paired with a personal commitment from the chair. For example, formal events on teaching went largely unattended by faculty, but if the chair taught—and taught well—faculty took notice. If chairs can demonstrate through these highly symbolic activities that teaching matters to them personally and therefore to the department, they will be better able to manage the meaning faculty make of departmental activities.

CHAPTER SIX

SHARING THE VALUE OF TEACHING:
WAYS TO BUILD A CULTURE OF CONGRUENCE

Imagine a stage on which several actors stand in the dark, dispersed across a stage. A spotlight highlights one: "I value teaching, but everyone else in my department doesn't!" The line is repeated as, one by one, each faculty member professes a value of teaching, yet an alienation from colleagues. Last, a chair is spotlighted: "How can I get my faculty to commit to our department's goals of valuing teaching?"

Unfortunately, this scene is not merely theatrical. In fact, it is enacted daily, as faculty in incongruent departments feel distanced from their colleagues, department, and institution.

What can faculty, chairs, and faculty developers do to instead create this scene? Imagine a stage on which several actors stand in the dark, spread apart across a stage. A spotlight highlights one: "I value teaching, and I think my department does, too." This faculty goes off to the other side of the stage, to talk to another actor about how her last class went. The line is repeated as, one by one, faculty members join colleagues in talking about pedagogy, watching each other's classes, and co-teaching. The chair is seen weaving amongst all of them, joining in a discussion here and a classroom there. Last, the whole stage is spotlighted, each faculty member speaking about, and listening to others, as all profess a value of teaching.

This concluding chapter takes a practical approach to suggest how university departments can construct a culture of congruence. Although this book is focused on teaching, conflict about the value of research, community outreach, service, or even diversity could just as easily divide a department, and readers in these other types of incongruent departments also may find the following suggestions useful. The first part of this chapter summarizes the key findings, while the second half draws practical conclusions for chairs and other members of a university community.

SUMMARY OF FINDINGS

In this book, I explore research university departments in which there is instructional congruence, or a culture in which individuals perceive that their beliefs about teaching align with their institution because department members have constructed shared understandings of effective teaching and the value they place on instruction.

Organizational congruence can benefit a department in a number of ways. Other research has established that it can reduce attrition, increase work satisfaction, and improve job performance. Here, I looked specifically at instructional congruence, and found that an aligned department had higher student ratings in its courses. Additionally, I suggested that congruence also may influence the long-term functioning of a department, increasing its institutional stability and enhancing faculty worklife for assistant professors.

Given these benefits, how do departments build cultures of congruence? In the case studies of the four departments presented here, several key elements emerged that involved an interaction between formal policy and faculty interpretations of those policies, as shaped through social interaction. Clear and transparent formal policies that facilitate discussion, practices and organizational structures that enable widespread faculty networks, and frequent communication between faculty and chairs enabled faculty to develop interpretive structures, or shared understandings and practices around values.

Incongruent departments were notable for the extent to which faculty did not construct shared interpretive structures of how to evaluate teaching, given the formal policies assigned to them by their departments and colleges. Faculty in these units established their own understandings of how organizational policy should be enacted; for example, it was common for faculty to feel that student ratings were invalid and instead that they should value only direct verbal feedback from students. However, these understandings predominantly were idiosyncratic and unsystematic. They relied upon a faculty member's individual sense of intuition or particular interactions with students and colleagues. For interpretive structures to have an impact on congruence, they must be shared.

Specifically, six organizational factors emerged in interviews as having the most impact on constructing faculty interaction patterns and enabling the development of interpretive structures. This "congruence checklist" includes:

1. *Instructional work:* How extensively is curricular work spread out through the department? Do many faculty teach introductory or service courses, or are these courses assigned to just a few instructors? Do faculty have an opportunity to teach together? Is team teaching sequential (i.e, "tag team teaching") or well integrated?

2. *Peer review:* Are there formal peer review procedures in place? If not, are there "performative" practices, or informal opportunities when colleagues can visit each others' classrooms?

3. *Instructional discussions:* Are discussions of teaching frequent and widespread?

4. *Practices for evaluating teaching:* Are practices locally validated? Do faculty take stock in the ways that teaching effectiveness is officially measured? Are there multiple means of assessing teaching effectiveness and student learning?

5. *Tenure and promotion policies for evaluating teaching:* Are instructional policies, especially for promotion and tenure, detailed and transparent? Do they promote interaction between faculty and administrators (e.g., peer review), in order to further clarify the policy?

6. *Attention to informal practices:* Is attention given to the interpretation of formal policies and events? Is discussion about teaching a taken-for-granted, everyday occurrence?

These six organizational elements appeared again and again in my interviews with faculty and administrators, as key factors that distinguished congruent from incongruent departments. (Two more will be added below, which focus on chairs' practice.) The following sections suggest practical strategies that administrators, faculty, faculty developers, and even future faculty can undertake to develop cultures of congruence.

Chairs

To return to the ideas presented in the previous chapter, department chairs face enormous pressures, both in terms of time and volume of workload. However, even within these constraints, many heads seek to create an aligned department culture. Utilizing the congruence checklist presented above, the following summary provides examples of what chairs can do to develop a culture of congruence. Many of these steps are relatively time-efficient, so that chairs do not have to choose between developing faculty or developing organizations.

1. *Distribute instructional work widely:* Administrators in congruent departments establish a plan for rotating the teaching among courses, so that many faculty teach service, required, or large courses. Similarly, curricular work is spread across the department. In creating this plan, service to these courses should be factored into annual reviews or tenure and promotion.

2. *Create peer review:* If feasible, team teaching can be integrated into the curriculum. If not, chairs can help to facilitate a peer observation program to allow faculty a window into each other's classrooms.

3. *Cultivate instructional discussions among faculty:* If desired, at events where all faculty are in attendance (e.g., beginning of the year meetings), chairs can place pedagogical discussions on the agenda to communicate the symbolic value the department accords to teaching. However, it may be more effective to establish very frequent informal events, such as conversations and coffee breaks, where teaching can be discussed.

4. *Develop practices for evaluating teaching:* With faculty input, chairs can establish multiple means of measuring teaching effectiveness and student learning.

5. *Clarify tenure and promotion policies for evaluating teaching:* Chairs should regularly talk with new faculty about what it means to be an "effective teacher," according to policies and local practices. Chairs also can observe faculty classrooms and discuss them with the instructors.

6. *Give attention to informal practices:* Through regular discussions with faculty, heads can better understand whether formal policies are well understood, formal teaching events well attended, and formal mechanisms for evaluating teaching well accepted. If any of these areas are found to be problematic, the strategies suggested above offer alternative paths.

Additionally, as discussed in the previous chapter, chairs' practices also had a great impact on the construction of a culture of congruence. Specifically, two other elements pertaining to chairs' leadership strategies should be added to the "congruence checklist":

7. *Initiate instructional discussions with faculty:* Congruent chairs talked with faculty about teaching on an informal, frequent basis. They also made "instructional field trips," going out of their office to talk with faculty, rather than waiting for faculty to come to them.

8. *Communicate symbolically the value of teaching:* Chairs in congruent departments carefully chose time-consuming, but highly meaningful, events that resonated with their faculty. These strategic activities communicated that the department values teaching because they involved a personal commitment to teaching on the part of the chair.

Other Key Players

The previous section looked at chairs as a key agent in constructing a culture of congruence. However, the role of other university actors should not be overlooked. Faculty, future faculty (i.e., job candidates), and faculty developers also are important actors in the process of constructing alignment around the value of teaching,

Faculty

While it falls within administrators' responsibilities to communicate organizational standards, it rests upon faculty's shoulders to translate these policies into workable procedures. Just as the congruence checklist was defined for chairs' activities, here, I suggest ways that faculty can play a key role in developing an aligned culture around teaching,

WHAT FACULTY CAN DO TO BUILD CONGRUENCE

- *Participate in instructional work and distribute it to others:* Faculty can offer their assistance in curricular design or instructional contributions to service courses. However, they also should be attuned to the concentration of this labor, seeking ways to draw others into pedagogical work and passing on their skills to younger faculty generations.

- *Observe peers:* Faculty can participate in (or construct) substantive team-teaching opportunities. If no formal process exists, informal visits among colleagues ("performative" evaluation) will also prove useful in establishing exchange of information about teaching.

- *Initiate instructional discussions with colleague:* An individual faculty member can help facilitate this process by seeking out conversations with colleagues and chairs about instructional issues, especially among those with whom one might not usually communicate. If there is a mentorship program, new faculty mentees can specifically request that their mentors address teaching (or seek out a mentor who is better situated to discuss instructional performance and evaluation).

- *Establish practices for evaluating teaching:* An important difference between congruent and incongruent departments that emerged was faculty's attitudes toward student and peer ratings, particularly the former. If faculty treat these evaluations as valid, they can be used to enhance instruction and communicate with colleagues about teaching. Faculty who do not find ratings to be valid need to reflectively think about what systematic mechanisms can complement or replace them in an evaluation portfolio. The third option—for faculty to believe student and peer evaluations to be invalid yet not substitute other regular mechanisms—results in an instructional void, which is filled by unsystematic measures such as gossip, intuition, and irregular word-of-mouth.

- *Clarify tenure and promotion policies for evaluating teaching:* Faculty can seek out chairs and experienced faculty to discuss what it means to be an "effective teacher," according to both policies and practice.

- *Pay attention to informal practices:* Faculty can help transform talk about teaching into a taken-for-granted everyday occurrence. Walk across the hall and ask a colleague how class went today; ask to learn more about another faculty member's style of teaching by visiting her class; or invite someone new to lunch to talk about instructional issues.

Finally, both faculty and administrators should be attuned to the emergence of possible isolates in the department. It is not necessary for everyone in a department to be a "pedagogical clone," or to think exactly identically about the value of teaching and how to measure effective instruction. However, faculty and administrators should build a repertoire of understandings about these issues. Exclusion of a few departmental members from these agreements can be extraordinarily detrimental to their careers and divisive to the department.

Future Faculty

Current graduate students should be aware that even though they may plan a career in a research university, they will spend a substantial amount of time on instruction, currently estimated at about 43.1 percent (private research universities) to 43.5 percent (public) of their total workload (Digest of Education Statistics, 2005). Additionally, future faculty should note the variety of forms of instructional work that they may be asked to perform: traditional classroom teaching, one-on-one work with students, and supervision of student research teams.

In looking for a faculty job, prospective professors would be advised to ask whether departments take steps to cultivate an instructional culture of congruence: How do they encourage clarity about tenure procedures? Who will mentor a new faculty member not only on research requirements but also on instructional standards? How much overlap among faculty do instructional arrangements involve? What do faculty talk about in the hall or at lunch? Finally, even if these questions are answered satisfactorily, there is the danger of being a marginal member in a congruent department. Applicants should steer away from positions in which the work scenario seems anomalous for the department, and they should be attuned to diversity issues. Danger signs for being marginal member may include a job location that lies outside of main department facilities, a job description where research or teaching responsibilities seem vastly different than other faculty's, or a department that does not fit the candidate's imagined diversity profile.

Faculty Developers

Programs that focus on instructional development of faculty often highlight workshops aimed toward individual faculty (e.g., how to lecture more effectively) rather than entire departments. Programs held in these formats are often, by definition, largely interdepartmental, and they often focus on the development of specific skills or techniques. Admittedly, a cultural approach to faculty and organizational development is more difficult, given the hidden, taken-for-granted nature of organizational environments (Sackmann, 1991). Programs that take a cultural focus may include initiatives to develop instructional networks, such as teaching circles (Cox, 1994), or grant monies for intradepartmental team teaching activity. Secondly, initiatives to train mentors to focus on faculty's instructional concerns, as well as their research-related questions, would help clarify institutional standards for new faculty. Finally, collaboration with academic leaders is an incredibly important arena, in order to support chairs' efforts to evaluate teaching, talk with faculty about teaching, and organize instructional work in the departments.

FUTURE RESEARCH

This research focused on four departments within one research university. Although this site was typical of this institutional type, further study on cultures of congruence would benefit from research in other universities. Just as I argue that there are important cultural variations within one research university, it is probably true that there are significant differences in policy and culture among research institutions that warrant further investigation. While research universities generally have been documented to have a culture of incongruence, it may be the case that some institutions do not fall within this pattern.

While this study treats departments with a culture of congruence as the exception for a research university, it would be informative to study other Carnegie types where alignment is expected for a majority of academic units. For example, a study of a liberal arts college may illustrate better what institutional policies (as opposed to department-level approaches) can contribute to congruence.

On a disciplinary level, this book focuses on one mega-discipline (the sciences), largely as an unintended outcome of the procedures used to select cases for further study. The advantages of this approach were that it facilitated comparison between the four case studies, lessening the chance that enormous variations in disciplinary orientations would occur. The clear disadvantage is that it may lessen the applicability of findings to other fields. A study that focused on a number of disciplinary types may provide useful qualifications to the findings presented here.

CONCLUSION

This research has explored how administrative actions and collegial interactions make it possible for colleagues to hold strikingly similar values about teaching. Conversely, where such informal networks are weak and policies are ill-communicated, faculty and administrators can hold strong individual opinions about the value of teaching, but their ideas and values seem to exist in isolation.

I approached my inquiry into the concept of congruence through encounters with several dedicated teachers I met during my graduate school career. Over the course of a year or so, I asked these faculty to attend a graduate student teaching group I helped to organize. As these discussions moved past the logistics of the group meeting to more in-depth narratives of their instructional experiences, I found many faculty relating some variation on the theme: "I value teaching, but I think [insert one or more of the following: my colleagues/this university/this department] do/does not." Sometimes I heard this from people who worked on the same hallway. How can it be, I wondered, that everyone feels alone in saying the same thing?

I was interested—and encouraged—to find during my inquiry that there are some research university departments that do not follow this pattern. Recent instructional reform movements have focused on changing the rewards structure at universities, with some increased awareness on the part of faculty and administrators, if not modest institutional changes. However, there has been little emphasis on the constructed meanings arising from existing personnel evaluation mechanisms. With greater attention to the need to cultivate a culture of instructional congruence, instructional reformers, faculty, and administrators can effect equally important benefits, namely a department that is conducive to instructional enhancement, faculty satisfaction, and a productive work environment.

APPENDIX A

FACULTY SEMI-STRUCTURED INTERVIEW INSTRUMENT

• Explain and distribute consent form.

Questions

• [For recommended faculty only] I know this is speculation on your part, but why do you think you were recommended to me as someone I should speak to about instructional issues?
• Instruction can happen in many contexts, such as work in the classroom or one-on-one work with students on a project. Can you describe your instructional activities for me?
• Thinking about all the things you do as a faculty member here at the university, about what percentage of time do you devote to these instructional activities you just named?
• What are things your department does that encourage you to spend time and effort on your instructional role, or that send a message that instruction is a valuable activity? The college or university?
• What are things your department does that discourage you to spend time on instructional activities, or that send a message that instruction is not a valuable activity? The college or university?
• If I were a new faculty member that stopped by your office, what advice would you give me about how to get tenure?
• [For assistant professors only] How did you learn these things yourself? Did you change how you allocated your time once you had learned these things?
• How long have you been working in this department? Over that time, what have you come to learn about what makes for a valued faculty member. [If interviewee asks, "Valued by whom?" respond, "The decision makers in the department."]
• The reason I ask about valued faculty is that in 1996, a survey was done of faculty in your department. X percent [fill in based on department's survey results] of faculty said that effective teaching is characteristic of a valued faculty member. Does this proportion surprise you or seem about right? [Prompt: If confused, ask, "If I were

to do a similar survey of faculty today, do you think I would see similar results?] Why?

- Also in the survey, X percent [fill in based on department's survey results] of faculty said that they, themselves, were effective teachers. Again, does this proportion surprise you or seem about right? Why do you think it was higher/lower/about the same?

- How does your department measure effective teaching? How do you know if someone is an effective teacher?

- When you want to talk to someone about teaching, with whom do you speak? Do most discussions about teaching in this department happen informally, or are there formal brownbags or colloquia?

- Is there anything I didn't ask you that I should have? Are there other people I should speak with who would have an interesting or valuable perspective on these issues?

APPENDIX B

1. Distribute consent form and respond to any questions regarding the form.

Common Questions

2. The role of the chair varies widely on this campus. Can you describe for me how you understand and carry out your duties as chair of this department? Who else helps make decisions in the department? Who are key people that make decisions about teaching, such as how teaching is evaluated? What kind of interactions do you have with the college around teaching issues (e.g., enrollment, curriculum)?

Tailored Questions

3. Now, I'd like to ask you about some findings I have gathered from my discussions with X [fill in number of faculty interviewed] faculty members in this department. Because I have promised them confidentiality, just as I promised you, I can not attribute these findings to particular individuals or even subgroups (e.g., junior faculty). What are your reactions to these findings?

[These questions varied by themes discovered in the four departments, treating topics such as:

• Things that encourage or discourage faculty to spend time on teaching

• How "effective teaching" is defined in the department generally, and for purposes of promotion/tenure

• What makes for a valued faculty member in the department

• Who are key actors around teaching in the department

• If and how instructional issues are discussed in the department

• The history of the department in relation to teaching]

NOTES

1. I ground the term *cultures of congruence* in the literature on organizational culture, which defines organizational culture as "the shared assumptions of individuals participating in organizations" (Tierney, 1988, p. 4.; see also Kuh & Whitt, 1988; Masland, 1985; and Tierney & Rhoads, 1993 for similar syntheses of the organizational culture research in higher education).

Palmer (1998) uses a similar term, "communities of congruence," but his usage differs from mine. His "communities of congruence" signifies a group of individuals who perceive institutional priorities as being in opposition to their own. This group offers "mutual support and opportunities to develop a shared vision" to change the institution (p. 166). I would argue that such a gathering describes a community of incongruence, because of the members' perceived opposition to institutional priorities. However, as I write in a later section, the formation of such a community is one important step in the construction of an eventual culture of congruence.

Another similar, but not identical concept to a culture of congruence is that of a "faculty learning community" (Cox & Richlin, 2004). However, the definition of a faculty learning community is different in that it is often cross-disciplinary and voluntary, and I focus on an intradepartmental work group. Second, although a faculty learning community certainly may develop shared beliefs about teaching, its primary function typically is more practice-oriented (Cox, 2004).

2. Interactive perspectives on organizations have been criticized for not explaining how organizational culture shapes social interactions to create an organizational climate (Moran & Volkwein, 1992). However, because I see congruence as a phenomenon of organizational culture (rather than climate), this criticism appears to be outside the scope of this study.

3. Only one Research II institution provided it as an option for tenure review.

4. It could be read that this measure indicates the value of teaching accorded by the individual and the department, rather than agreement about definitions of effective teaching. However, in interviews, respondents were very clear that their reading of the question favored the latter interpretation. They felt strongly that one's value of teaching and one's instructional effectiveness were distinct issues.

5. The number six was arbitrary, as the selection process described below moves from the top in ruling out departments from the study.

6. This quantity of interviews is well above accepted standards for qualitative research studies (Guest, Bunce, & Johnson, 2006).

7. These departments happened to be matched on Biglan (1973) dimensions.

8. It may be that some students took courses in both departments, which also would violate the assumption of independence. Because the student evaluations are

anonymously completed, it is impossible to determine the overlap. However, the effect is probably minimal.

9. There was one additional junior faculty member I interviewed who had an appointment in one of the departments of interest, but his/her primary instructional work and appointment was located in another department. As a result, I did not ask this person about the survey results because I felt s/he did not have enough experience in the department to adequately respond to the question.

10. This literature should be distinguished from many studies termed "person-environment," which often focus on the intersection between personality and vocation or job (e.g., Holland, 1985 and Betz, 1987).

11. See also Kuh and Whitt (1988), Masland (1985), and Tierney and Rhoads (1993) for similar syntheses of the organizational culture literature in higher education and, for a general definition, Ouchi and Wilkins (1985).

12. Ryan and Schmitt's (1996) research on an insurance firm also describes an organization in which there was overall organizational congruence, but subcultures of members with more similar beliefs existed as well.

13. Wenger and Snyder's (2000) concept of communities of practice differs from both the formal department organization and the informal teaching networks I discuss here. However, Lattuca (2002) studies the communities of practice developed by interdisciplinary teachers.

14. Sometimes, respondents mentioned names of colleagues whom they felt held interesting views about teaching because they did not value instruction, and these references are included because they serve as a negative standard. In other words, these colleagues were a model for the respondent of what not to do or believe as an instructor.

REFERENCES

Aleamoni, L. M. (1987). Typical faculty concerns about student evaluation of teaching. In *New directions for teaching and learning, 31* (pp. 25–31). San Francisco: Jossey-Bass.

Alicke, M. D. (1985). Global self-evaluation as determined by the desirability and controllability of trait adjectives. *Journal of Personality and Social Psychology, 49,* 1621–1630.

Arreola, R. A. (2000). *Developing a comprehensive faculty evaluation system: A handbook for college faculty and administrators on designing and operating a comprehensive faculty evaluation system* (2nd ed.). Bolton, MA: Anker.

Astin, A. (1993). *What matters in college? Four critical years revisited.* San Francisco: Jossey-Bass.

Astin, A. W., Korn, W. S., & Dey, E. L. (1991). *The American college teacher: National norms for the 1989–90 HERI Faculty Survey.* Higher Education Research Institute, Los Angeles.

Basow, S. A. (1998). Student evaluations: Gender bias and teaching styles. In L. H. Collins, J. C. Chrisler, & K. Quina (Eds.), *Career strategies for women in academe: Arming Athena* (pp. 135–156). Thousand Oaks, CA: Sage.

Bechhofer, S., & Barnhart, B. (1999). Learning from leavers. In R. J. Menges (Ed.), *Faculty in new jobs: A guide to settling in, becoming established, and building institutional support* (pp. 291–309). San Francisco: Jossey-Bass.

Bess, J. L. (2000). *Teaching alone, teaching together: Transforming the structure of teams for teaching.* San Francisco: Jossey-Bass.

Betz, N. E., Ed. (1987). *Journal of Vocational Behavior. Special Edition: Conceptual and Methodological Issues in Person-Environment Fit Research, 31.*

Biglan, A. (1973). Relationships between subject matter characteristics and structure and output of university departments. *Journal of Applied Psychology, 57,* 204–213.

Bilimoria, D., & Jordan, C. G. (2005). A good place to do science: An exploratory case study of an academic science department. Paper presentation at the NSF-ADVANCE meeting, Washington, D.C. Available: http://www.case.edu/admin/aces/resources.htm

Blackburn, R. T., Boberg, A., O'Connell, C., & Pellino, G. (1980). *Project for faculty development program evaluation, final report.* Ann Arbor, MI: Center for the Study of Higher Education.

Blackburn, R. T., & Lawrence, J. H. (1995). *Faculty at work: Motivation, expectation, satisfaction.* Baltimore: Johns Hopkins University Press.

Bland, C. J., Weber-Main, A. M., Lund, S. M., & Finstad, D. A. (2005). *The research-productive department: Strategies from departments that excel.* Bolton, MA: Anker.

Blau, P. M. (1973). *The organization of academic work.* New York: Wiley.

Boice, R. (1991). New faculty as teachers. *Journal of Higher Education, 62,* 150–173.

Boice, R. (1992). *The new faculty member: Supporting and fostering professional development.* San Francisco: Jossey-Bass.

Boice, R. (1993a). Early turning points in professorial careers of women and minorities. In J. Gainen and R. Boice (Eds.), *New directions for teaching and learning: Building a diverse faculty, 53* (pp. 71–79). San Francisco: Jossey-Bass.

Boice, R. (1993b). New faculty involvement for women and minorities. *Research in Higher Education, 34,* 291–341.

Bolman, L. G., & Deal, T. E. (2003). *Reframing organizations: Artistry, choice, and leadership.* San Francisco: Jossey-Bass.

Boyer, E. L. (1990). *Scholarship reconsidered: Priorities of the professoriate.* Princeton: The Carnegie Foundation for the Advancement of Teaching.

Braxton, J. M., & Berger, J. B. (1999). How disciplinary consensus affects faculty. In R. J. Menges (Ed.), *Faculty in new jobs: A guide to settling in, becoming established, and building institutional support* (pp. 243–267). San Francisco: Jossey-Bass.

Braxton, J. M., & Hargens, L. L. (1996). Variation among academic disciplines: Analytical frameworks and research. In J. C. Smart (Ed.), *Higher education: Handbook of theory and research* (Vol. 11, pp. 1–46). New York: Agathon Press.

Braxton, J. M., Bayer, A. E., & Finkelstein, M. J. (1992). Teaching performance norms in academia. *Research in Higher Education, 33,* 533–569.

Burt, R. S. (1980). Models of network structure. *Annual Review of Sociology, 6,* 79–141.

Campbell, J. (1986). Similarity and uniqueness: The effects of attribute type, relevance, and individual differences in self-esteem and depression. *Journal of Personality and Social Psychology, 50,* 281–294.

Cantor, N., & Lavine, D. D. (2006, June 9). Taking public scholarship seriously. *Chronicle of Higher Education, 52(40),* B52.

Caplow, T., & McGee, R. J. (1961 [1958]). *The academic marketplace.* New York: Science Editions.

Carnegie Commission on Higher Education. (1973). *A classification of institutions of higher education: A technical report.* Berkeley.

Carroll, J. B., & Gmelch, W. H. (1994). Department chair's perceptions of the relative importance of their duties. *Journal for Higher Education Management, 10(1),* 49–63.

Cashin, W. E. (1990). Students do rate different academic fields differently. In M. Theall & J. Franklin (Eds.), *New directions for teaching and learning: Student ratings of instruction: Issues for improving practice, 43* (pp. 113–121). San Francisco: Jossey-Bass.

Cashin, W. E. (1995). *Student ratings of teaching: The research revisited.* IDEA Paper, No. 32. Center for Faculty Evaluation and Development, Kansas State University. Available online: http://www.idea.ksu.edu/papers/Idea_Paper_32.pdf

Charmaz, K. (1983). The grounded theory method: An explanation and interpretation. In R. M. Emerson (Ed.), *Contemporary field research: A collection of readings* (pp. 109–126). Boston: Little, Brown.

Chatman, J. A. (1989). Improving interactional organizational research: A model of person-organization fit. *Academy of Management Review, 14,* 333–349.

Chatman, J. A. (1991). Matching people and organizations: Selection and socialization in public accounting firms. *Administrative Science Quarterly, 36,* 459–484.

Chatman, J. A., & Barsade, S. G. (1995). Personality, organizational culture, and cooperation: Evidence from a business simulation. *Administrative Science Quarterly, 40,* 423–432.

Chatman, J. A., Polzer, J. T., Barsade, S. A., & Neale. M. A. (1998). Being different yet feeling similar: The influence of demographic composition and organizational culture on work processes and outcomes. *Administrative Science Quarterly, 43(4),* 749–780.

Chesler, M. (1987). *Professional's views of the "dangers" of self-help groups.* Ann Arbor: Center for Research on Social Organization, University of Michigan.

Clark, B. R. (1987). *The academic life: Small worlds, different worlds.* Princeton: Carnegie Foundation for the Advancement of Teaching.

Clark, C. M., & Peterson, P. L. (1986). Teachers' thought processes. In M. C. Wittrock (Ed.), *Handbook of research in teaching* (pp. 255–296). New York: MacMillan.

Colbeck, C. (1994). *The contexts of academic work: What matters to faculty.* Paper presented at the Annual Meeting for the Association for the Study of Higher Education. Tucson, AZ.

Committee on Science, Engineering and Public Policy. (2006). *Rising above the gathering storm: Energizing and employing America for a brighter economic future.* Washington, DC: The National Academy of Sciences, The National Academy of Engineering, and The Institute of Medicine. Available online: http://www.nap.edu/catalog/11463.html

Cook, S. D. N., & Yanow, D. (1995). Culture and organizational learning. In M. D. Cohen & L. Sproull (Eds.), *Organizational learning* (pp. 430–459). Newbury Park, CA: Sage.

Corbin, J., & Strauss, A. L. (1990). Grounded theory research: Procedures, canons, and evaluative criteria. *Qualitative Sociology, 13,* 3–21.

Cox, M. D. (2004). Introduction to faculty learning communities. In M. D. Cox & L. Richlin (Eds.), *New directions for teaching and learning: Building faculty learning communities, 97* (pp. 5–23). San Francisco: Jossey-Bass.

Cox, M. D., & Richlin, L. (Eds.) (2004). *New directions for teaching and learning: Building faculty learning communities, 97.* San Francisco: Jossey-Bass.

Cuban, L. (1999). *How scholars trumped teachers: Change without reform in university curriculum, teaching, and research, 1890–1990.* New York: Teachers College Press.

Davis, K. S. (2001). "Peripheral and subversive": Women making connections and challenging the boundaries of the science community. *Science Education, 85,* 368–409.

Denzin, N. K. (1978). *A theoretical introduction to sociological methods.* New York: McGraw-Hill.

Diamond, R. M., & Adam, B. E. (1997). *Changing priorities at research universities: 1991–1996.* Syracuse: Center for Instructional Development, Syracuse University.

Dubrow, G., Moseley, B., & Dustin, D. (2006). Life at Mission Creep U. *Academe, 92(3).* Available online: http://www.aaup.org/publications/Academe/2006/06mj/06mjdubrsneak.htm

Dunning, D., Meyerowitz, J. A., & Holzberg, A. D. (1989). Ambiguity and self-evaluation: The role of idiosyncratic trait definitions in self-serving assessments of ability. *Journal of Personality and Social Psychology, 57,* 1082–1090.

Edwards, R. (1999). The academic department: How does it fit into the university reform agenda? *Change*, *31(5)*, 17.

Erickson, B. H. (1988). The relational basis of attitudes. In B. Wellman & S. D. Berkowitz (Eds.), *Social structures: A network approach* (pp. 99–121). Cambridge: Cambridge University Press.

Etzkowitz, H., Kemelgor, C., & Uzzi, B. (2000). *Athena unbound: The advancement of women in science and technology*. Cambridge: Cambridge University Press.

Fairweather, J. A., & Rhoads, R. A. (1995). Teaching and the faculty role: Enhancing the commitment to instruction in American colleges and universities. *Educational Evaluation and Policy Analysis*, *17*, 179–194.

Feldman, K. A. (1979). The significance of circumstances for college students' ratings of their teachers and courses. *Research in Higher Education*, *10(2)*, 149–172.

Feldman, K. A. (1983). Seniority and experience of college teachers as related to evaluations they receive from students. *Research in Higher Education*, *18(1)*, 3–124.

Feldman, K. A. (1992). College students' views of male and female college teachers: Part I—Evidence from the social laboratory and experiments. *Research in higher education*, *33*, 317–375.

Feldman, K. A. (1993). College students' views of male and female college teachers: Part II—Evidence from students' evaluations of their classroom teachers. *Research in Higher Education*, *34*, 151–191.

Feldman, K. A., & Paulsen, M. B. (1999). Faculty motivation: The role of a supportive teaching culture. *New Directions for Teaching and Learning*, *78*, 71–78.

Fink, D. L. (1984). *New directions for teaching and learning: The first year of college teaching*, *17*. San Francisco: Jossey-Bass.

Finkelstein, M. J. (1984). *The American academic profession: A synthesis of social scientific inquiry since World War II*. Columbus: Ohio State University Press.

Finkelstein, M. J., Seal, R. K., & Schuster, J. H. (1998). *The new academic generation: A profession in transformation*. Baltimore: Johns Hopkins University Press.

Franklin, E. (2005, October 6). Interim and tenured. *Chronicle of Higher Education: Chronicle Careers*. Available: http://chronicle.com/jobs/2005/10/2005100601c.htm

Franklin, J., & Theall, M. (1990). Communicating student ratings to decision makers: Design for good practice. In M. Theall & J. Franklin (Eds.), *New directions for teaching and learning: Student ratings of instruction: Issues for improving practice*, *43*. San Francisco: Jossey-Bass.

Friedkin, N. (1978). University social structure and social networks among scientists. *American Journal of Sociology*, *83*, 1444–1465.

Gartrell, C. D. (1987). Network approaches to social evaluation. *Annual Review of Sociology*, *13*, 49–66.

Glaser, B. G. (1987). *Theoretical sensitivity: Advances in the methodology of grounded theory*. Mill Valley, CA: Sociology Press.

Glaser, B. G, & Strauss, A. L. (1967). *The discovery of grounded theory: Strategies for qualitative research*. New York: Aldine De Gruyter.

Goodwin, L. D., & Stevens, E. A. (1993). The influence of gender on university faculty members' perceptions of "good" teaching. *Journal of Higher Education*, *64*, 166–185.

Goethals, G. R. (1986). Fabricating and ignoring social reality: Self-serving estimates of consensus. In J. M. Olson, C. P. Herman, & M. P. Zanna (Eds.), *Relative deprivation and social comparison: The Ontario symposium* (Vol. 4, pp. 135–157). Lawrence Erlbaum Associates.

Gouldner, A. W. (1957). Cosmopolitans and locals: Toward an analysis of latent social roles. *Administrative Science Quarterly, 2,* 244–306.

Guest, G., Bunce, A., & Johnson, L. (2006). How many interviews are enough?: An experiment with data saturation and variability. *Field Methods, 18(1),* 59–82.

Hecht, I. W. D., Higgerson, M. L., Gmelch, W. H., & Tucker, A. (1999). *The department chair as academic leader.* Phoenix: American Council on Higher Education and Onyx Press.

Helgeson, S. (1995). *The web of inclusion: A new architecture for building great organizations.* New York: Doubleday.

Hofer, B. K., & Brown, D. R. (1992). *The relative importance of research and undergraduate teaching.* Ann Arbor: Center for Research on Learning and Teaching, University of Michigan.

Holland, J. (1985). *Making vocational choices: A theory of careers.* Englewood Cliffs, NJ.: Prentice-Hall.

Hutchings, P., & Shulman, L. S. (1999). The scholarship of teaching and learning: New elaborations, new developments. *Change,31(5),* 10–15.

Johnsrud, L. K. & Wunsch, M. (1991). Junior and senior faculty women: Commonalities and differences in perceptions of academic life. *Psychological Reports* 69, 879–886.

Kanter, R. M. (1977). *Men and women of the corporation.* New York: Basic Books.

Kardia, D. K., & Wright, M. (2004). *Instructor identity: The impact of gender and race on faculty experiences with teaching.* CRLT Occasional Paper, No. 19. Ann Arbor: Center for Research on Learning and Teaching, University of Michigan. Available: http://www.crlt.umich.edu

Kesar, A. (2005). Moving from I to we: Reorganizing for collaboration in higher education. *Change, 37(6),* 50–58.

Krebs, P. M. (2005, September 23). Colleges focused on teaching too often neglect research. *Chronicle of Higher Education, 52(5),* B14.

Kristof-Brown, A. L., Zimmerman, R. D., & Johnson, E. C. (2005). Consequences of individuals' fit at work: A meta-analysis of person-job, person-organization, person-group, and person-supervisor fit. *Personnel Psychology, 58(2),* 281–342.

Kuh, G. D., & Whitt, E. J. (1988). *The invisible tapestry: Culture in American colleges and universities.* College Station, TX: Association for the Study of Higher Education.

Lattuca, L. R. (2002). Learning interdisciplinarily: Sociocultural perspectives on academic work. *The Journal of Higher Education, 73(6),* 711–739.

Lattuca, L. R., & Stark, J. S. (1995). Modifying the major: Discretionary thoughts from ten disciplines. *Review of Higher Education,18,* 315–344.

Lawrence, J. H. (1984). Faculty age and teaching. *New directions for teaching and learning: Teaching and aging, 19,* 57–65.

Lees, N. D. (2006). *Chairing academic departments: Traditional and emerging expectations.* Bolton, MA.: Anker.

Leslie, D. W. (2002). Resolving the dispute: Teaching is academe's core value. *Journal of Higher Education, 73,* 49–73.

Lincoln, Y. S. & Guba, E. G. (1985). *Naturalistic inquiry.* Beverly Hills: Sage.

Lindholm, J. A. (2003). Perceived organizational fit: Nurturing the minds, hearts, and personal ambitions of university faculty. *The Review of Higher Education,27,* 125–149.

Louis, M. R. (1980). Surprise and sense making: What newcomers experience in entering unfamiliar organizational settings. *Administrative Science Quarterly, 25*, 226–251.

Lucas, A. H. (1989). Motivating faculty to improve the quality of teaching. *New directions for teaching and learning, 27*, 5–16.

Lucas, A. H. (1990). The department chair as change agent. In P. Seldin (Ed.), *How administrators can improve teaching: Moving from talk to action in higher education.* San Francisco: Jossey-Bass.

Mallard, K. S. (1999). Management by walking around and the department chair. *The Department Chair, 10(2),* 13.

Manis, J. D., Thomas, N. G., Sloat, B. F., & Davis, C. G. (1989). *Factors affecting choices of majors in science, mathematics, and engineering at the University of Michigan.* Ann Arbor: Center for the Continuing Education of Women.

Mann, R. D. (1970). *The college classroom: Conflict, change, and learning.* New York: J. Wiley.

March, J. (1982). *Emerging developments in the study of organizations.* Paper presented at the Annual Meeting for the Study of Higher Education, Washington, DC.

March, J. G., & Olsen, J. P. (1976). *Ambiguity and choice in organizations.* Bergen, Germany: Universitetsforlaget.

Marcus, D. L. (1999, August 30). The big are getting bigger: Research universities are working to put undergraduates first. *U.S. News and World Report,* p. 66.

Markin, K. (2005, November 25). If you're a scientist who is not used to collaborating with nonscientists, you'd better get used to it. *Chronicle of Higher Education, 52(14),* C3.

Marks, G., & Miller, N. (1987). Ten years of research on the false-consensus effect: An empirical and theoretical review. *Psychological Bulletin,102,* 72–90.

Marsden, P. V., & Friedkin, N. H. (1994). Network studies of social influence. In S. Wasserman & J. Galaskiewicz (Eds.), *Advances in social network analysis: Research in the social and behavioral sciences* (pp. 3–25). Thousand Oaks, CA: Sage.

Marsh, H. W. (1987). Students' evaluation of university teaching: Research findings, methodological issues, and directions for future research. *International Journal of Educational Research, 11,* 253–388.

Marsh, H. W., & Roche, L. A. (1997). Making students' evaluation of teaching effectiveness effective: The critical issues of validity, bias, and utility. *American Psychologist, 52(11),* 1187–1197.

Masland, A. T. (1985). Organizational culture in the study of higher education. *Review of Higher Education, 8,* 157–168.

Massy, W. F., Wilger, A. K., & Colbeck, C. (1994). Overcoming "hollowed" collegiality. *Change, 26,* 11–20.

McCaskey, M. B. (1982). *The executive challenge: Managing change and ambiguity.* Marshfield, MA: Pitman.

Menges, R. J. (1999). Dilemmas of newly hired faculty. In R. J. Menges (Ed.), *Faculty in new jobs: A guide to settling in, becoming established, and building institutional support* (pp. 19–38). San Francisco: Jossey-Bass.

Miller, D. T., & McFarland, C. (1987). Pluralistic ignorance: When similarity is interpreted as dissimilarity. *Journal of Personality and Social Psychology,53,* 298–305.

Miller, D. T., & Prentice, D. A. (1996). The construction of social norms and standards. In E. T. Higgins (Ed.), *Social psychology: Handbook of basic principles* (pp. 799–829). New York: The Guilford Press.

Moran, E. T., & Volkwein, J. F. (1992). The cultural approach to the formation of organizational climate. *Human Relations, 45(1),* 19–47.

Moreno, J. L. (1934). *Who shall survive? A new approach to the problem of human interrelations.* Washington, DC: Nervous and Mental Disease Publishing Co.

National Center for Education Statistics (2005). *Digest of education statistics.* (NSOPF:04). Washington, DC: U.S. Department of Education.

Olsen, D., Maple, S. A., & Stage, F. K. (1995). Women and minority job satisfaction: Professional role interests, professional satisfactions, and institutional fit. *Journal of Higher Education, 66,* 267–293.

O'Meara, K. (2000). Climbing the academic ladder: Promotion in rank. In C. A. Trower (Ed.), *Policies on faculty appointment: Standard practices and unusual arrangements* (pp. 141–179). Bolton, MA: Anker.

O'Meara, K. (2003). Believing is seeing: The influence of beliefs and expectations on posttenure review in one state system. *The Review of Higher Education, 27(1),* 17–43.

O'Reilly III, C., & Chatman, J. (1986). Organizational commitment and psychological attachment: The effects of compliance, identification, and internalization on prosocial behavior. *Journal of Applied Psychology, 71,* 492–499.

O'Reilly, C. A., Chatman, J., & Caldwell, D. F. (1991). People and organizational culture: A profile comparison approach to assessing person-organization fit. *Academy of Management Journal, 34,* 487–516.

Ory, J. C. (2001). Faculty thoughts and concerns about student ratings. In K. G. Lewis (Ed.), *New Directions for Teaching and Learning: Techniques and Strategies for Interpreting Student Evaluations, 87* (pp. 3–15). San Francisco: Jossey Bass.

Ory. J. C., & Ryan, C. (2002). How do student ratings measure up to a new validity framework? In M. Theall, P. C. Abrami, & L. A. Mets (Eds.), *New directions for institutional research: The student ratings debate: Are they valid? How can we best use them?, 2001(109)* (pp. 27–44). San Francisco: Jossey-Bass.

Ostroff, C., & Routhausen, T. J. (1997). The moderating effect of tenure in person-environment fit: A field study in educational organizations. *Journal of Occupational and Organizational Psychology, 70,* 173–188.

Ouchi, W. G., & Wilkins, A. G. (1985). Organizational culture. *Annual Review of Sociology,11,* 457–483.

Palmer, P. J. (1998). *The courage to teach: Exploring the inner landscape of a teacher's life.* San Francisco: Jossey-Bass.

Paulsen, M. B., & Feldman, K. A. (1995). *Taking teaching seriously: Meeting the challenge of instructional improvement.* (ASHE-ERIC Higher Education Report, No. 2). Washington, DC: The George Washington University, Graduate School of Education and Human Development.

Peters, D. S., & Mayfield, R. J. (1982). Are there any rewards for teaching? *Improving College and University Teaching, 30,* 105–110.

Poole, M. S., & McPhee., R. D. (1983). A structurational analysis of organizational culture. In L. L. Putnam & M. E. Pacanowsky (Eds.), *Communication and organizations: An interpretive approach* (pp. 195–220). Beverly Hills: Sage.

Pope, L. (1996). *Colleges that change lives: 40 schools you should know about even if you're not a straight-A student*. New York: Penguin Books.

Quinlan, K. M. (1996). *Collaboration and cultures of teaching in university departments: Faculty beliefs about teaching and learning in history and engineering*. Unpublished doctoral dissertation, Stanford University.

Quinn, J. W. (1994). *A norm for teaching development: Faculty perceptions at five institutions*. Unpublished doctoral dissertation, Northwestern University.

Ragin, C. C., Nagel, J., & White, P. (2004). *Workshop on scientific foundations of qualitative research*. Washington, DC: National Science Foundation.

Rice, R. E., & Austin, A. (1990). Organizational impacts on faculty morale and motivation to teach. In Seldin, P. (Ed.), *How administrators can improve teaching: Moving from talk to action in higher education*. San Francisco: Jossey-Bass.

Rohrer, J. D. (1997). *A retrospective study of how new faculty report the use of mentoring relationships to make sense of their multiple roles*. PhD dissertation. Michigan State University.

Rose, S. (1989). Women biologists and the "old boy" network. *Women's Studies International Forum, 12*, 349–354.

Ryan, A. M., & Schmitt, M. J. (1996). An assessment of organizational climate and P-E fit: A tool for organizational change. *International Journal of Organizational Analysis, 4(1)*, 75–95.

Sackmann, S. A. (1991). Uncovering culture in organizations. *Journal of Applied Behavioral Science, 27*, 295–317.

Sax, L. J., Astin, A., Korn, W. S., & Gilmartin, S. K. (1999). *The American college teacher: National norms for the 1998–99 HERI faculty survey*. Los Angeles: Higher Education Research Institute.

Schuster, J. H., & Finkelstein, M. J. (2006). *The American faculty: The restructuring of academic work and careers*. Baltimore: The Johns Hopkins University Press.

Scott, J. (2000). *Social network analysis: A handbook*. Thousand Oaks, CA: Sage.

Seagren, A. Y., Creswell, J. W., & Wheeler, D. W. (1993). *The department as chair: New roles, responsibilities and challenges* (ASHE-ERIC Higher Ed Report No. 1). Washington, DC: School of Education and Human Development, George Washington University.

Seldin, P. (1990). Academic environments and teaching effectiveness. In P. Seldin (Ed.), *How administrators can improve teaching: Moving from talk to action in higher education* (pp. 3–22). San Francisco: Jossey-Bass.

Seldin, P. (Ed.).(1999). *Changing practices in evaluating teaching: A practical guide to improved faculty performance and promotion/tenure decisions*. Bolton, MA.: Anker.

Senge, P. M. (1990). *The fifth discipline*. New York: Doubleday.

Senge, P. M. (2000). The academy as learning community: Contradiction in terms or realizable future? In A. E. Lucas (Ed.), *Leading academic change: Essential roles for academic change* (pp. 275–300). San Francisco: Jossey-Bass.

Sewell Jr., W. H. (1992). A theory of structure: Duality, agency, and transformation. *American Journal of Sociology, 98(1)*, 1–29.

Seymour, E., & Hewitt, N. M. (1997). *Talking about leaving: Why undergraduates leave the sciences*. Boulder: Westview Press.

Singer, J. E. (1980). Social comparison: The process of self-evaluation. In L. Festinger (Ed.), *Retrospections on social psychology* (pp. 158–179). Oxford: Oxford University Press.

Smircich, L., & Morgan, G. (1983). Leadership: The management of meaning. *Journal of Applied Behavioral Science, 18*(3), 257–273.

Sonnert, G. (1995). *Gender differences in the sciences: The Project Access Study.* New Brunswick: Rutgers University Press.

Sykes, C. J. (1988). *ProfScam: Professors and the demise of higher education.* Washington, DC: Regnery Gateway.

Thaves, B. (2004, January 31). *Frank and Ernest*, appearing in the Ann Arbor News, B6.

Tierney, W. G. (1988). Organizational culture in higher education: Defining the essentials. *Journal of Higher Education, 59*, 2–21

Tierney, W. G., & Bensimon, E. M. (1996). *Promotion and tenure: Community and socialization in academe.* Albany: State University of New York Press.

Tierney, W. G., & Rhoads, R. A. (1993). *Enhancing promotion, tenure, and beyond: Faculty socialization as a cultural process.* ASHE-ERIC Higher Education Report, No. 6. Washington, DC.

Tobias, S. (1990). *They're not dumb, they're different: Stalking the second tier.* Tucson: Research Corporation.

Traweek, S. (1998). *Beamtimes and lifetimes: The world of high energy physicists.* Cambridge: Harvard University Press.

Trotter II, R. T. (1999). Friends, relatives, and relevant others: Conducting ethnographic network studies. In J. J. Schensul & M. D. LeCompte (Eds.), *Mapping social networks, spacial data, and hidden populations*, 4 (pp. 1–50). Walnut Creek, CA: Altamira.

Trout, P. A. (1997). What the numbers mean. *Change, 29*(5), 24–31.

Van Lange, P. A. (1991). Being better but not smarter than others: The Muhammed Ali effect at work on interpersonal situations. *Personality and Social Psychology Bulletin, 17*, 689–693.

Verquer, M. L., Beehr, T. A., & Wagner, S. H. (2002). A meta-analysis of relations between person-organization fit and work attitudes. *Journal of Vocational Behavior, 63*, 473–489.

Weick, K. E. (1979a). Cognitive processes in organizations. In B. M. Staw (Ed.), *Research in organizational behavior,*1 (pp. 41–74). Greenwich, CT: JAI Press.

Weick, K. E. (1979b). *The social psychology of organizing.* Reading, MA: Addison-Wesley.

Weick, K. E. (1995). *Sensemaking in organizations.* Thousand Oaks, CA: Sage Publications.

Wenger, E. C., & Snyder, W. M. (2000, January–February). Communities of practice: The organizational frontier. *Harvard Business Review,* 139–145.

Wergin, J. F. (2003). *Departments that work: Building and sustaining cultures of excellence in academic programs.* Bolton, MA: Anker.

Whitt, E. J. (1991). Hit the ground running: Experiences of new faculty in a school of education. *Review of Higher Education, 14*, 177–197.

Wilson, R. (2002, October 18). Bickering decimates a department. *The Chronicle of Higher Education, 49*(8), A12.

Wood, M., & Des Jarlais, C. (2006). When post-tenure review policy and practice diverge: Making the case for congruence. *Journal of Higher Education, 77*(4), 561–588.

Woods, J. Q. (1999). Establishing a teaching development culture. In R. J. Menges (Ed.), *Faculty in new jobs: A guide to settling in, becoming established, and building institutional support* (pp. 268–290). San Francisco: Jossey-Bass.

Wright, M., Howery, C., Assar, N., McKinney, K., Kain, E. L., Glass, B., Kramer, L., & Atkinson, M. (2004). Greedy institutions: The importance of institutional context for teaching in higher education. *Teaching Sociology, 23(2)*, 144–159.

Wright, M. C. (2002). *Always at odds? Faculty beliefs about teaching at a research university.* Unpublished doctoral dissertation. University of Michigan, Ann Arbor, Michigan.

Yanow, D. (2000). Seeing organizational learning: A "cultural" view. *Organization, 7(2)*, 247–268.

INDEX